Caring for All Creatures

Caring for All Creatures

The Ethics of Animal Welfare

Rafeal Mechlore

Leader Enterprises

CONTENTS

INDEX

Introduction

1. The importance of animal welfare in today's society
2. The moral and ethical foundations of caring for animals
3. The scope of the book and its objectives

Chapter 1 Historical Perspectives on Animal Welfare
1.1 Ancient civilizations and their attitudes toward animals
1.2 The role of religion and philosophy in shaping our views on animals
1.3 Early animal protection movements and their impact on society

Chapter 2 The Science of Animal Welfare
2.1 Understanding animal behavior and emotions
2.2 The role of animal cognition in ethical considerations
2.3 The impact of stress, pain, and suffering on animals

Chapter 3 Ethical Frameworks for Animal Welfare
3.1 Utilitarianism and its application to animal ethics
3.2 Deontology and its implications for animal rights
3.3 Virtue ethics and the cultivation of empathy for animals

Chapter 4 Animal Rights and Legal Protections
4.1 The history of animal rights movements
4.2 The development of animal welfare laws and regulations
4.3 Contemporary debates on animal personhood and legal rights

Chapter 5 The Ethics of Animal Use
5.1 The ethics of factory farming and industrial agriculture
5.2 Animal testing and its moral implications
5.3 The ethics of using animals in entertainment and sports

INTRODUCTION

In a world portrayed by its interconnectedness and a developing consciousness of our common obligations towards each other, there exists an ethical basic to expand our sympathy and moral contemplations past the limits of our own species. This significant moral commitment calls us to look at the perplexing and multi-layered domain of creature government assistance — a space wherein our activities, as people, significantly affect the lives and prosperity of innumerable animals that share our planet. "Really focusing on All Animals: The Morals of Creature Government assistance" sets out on a provocative excursion, crossing north of 2000 words, to investigate the major inquiries and moral quandaries encompassing our treatment of non-human creatures. In this investigation, we dig into the verifiable setting of our relationship with creatures, the rules that underlie our moral contemplations, and the reasonable ramifications of these qualities in our cutting edge world.

The historical backdrop of humankind's connection with creatures is just about as old as our own reality. As we follow the development of our relationship with different animals, we experience a rich embroidery of communications, spreading over from the taming of creatures for horticulture and friendship to the double-dealing of untamed life for game and diversion. Over this course, our treatment of creatures has differed broadly, thinking about both our reliance them for endurance and our affinity for remorselessness, lack of concern, and double-dealing.

Early human social orders depended intensely on creatures for food, involving them as wellsprings of food, work, and attire. The endurance of these social orders was inseparably connected to their capacity to really oversee and use creatures. In any case, as human social orders developed and turned out to be all the more mechanically progressed, our reliance on creatures for getting through one day to the next reduced, leading to new moral contemplations.

The rise of reasoning and moral frameworks further refined how we might interpret our relationship with creatures. Antiquated Greek thinkers like Pythagoras and Plato supported for the moral treatment of creatures, perceiving their consciousness and limit with respect to affliction. These early philosophical experiences established the groundwork for future conversations on creature government assistance and our ethical constraints toward them.

In later hundreds of years, the Modern Transformation and advances in science prompted sensational changes in our relationship with creatures. The development of manufacturing plant cultivating, specifically, brought up new moral issues. As creatures were progressively treated as items, worries about their day to day environments, wellbeing, and government assistance started to acquire unmistakable quality. Early creature government assistance developments arose, supporting for compassionate treatment and better day to day environments for creatures in farming and different ventures.

The twentieth century saw a critical change in cultural perspectives toward creatures. The distribution of Rachel Carson's notable book "Quiet Spring" and the natural development of the 1960s featured the interconnectedness of every living being and the delicate equilibrium of our biological systems. These improvements underlined the requirement for a more caring and biologically feasible way to deal with creature government assistance.

Today, our moral contemplations encompassing creatures keep on developing. We wind up wrestling with significant inquiries regarding the ethical status of creatures, the privileges they might be qualified for, and our obligations as stewards of the planet. How we might interpret creature discernment and consciousness has extended, uncovering the intricacy of their internal lives and the limit with respect to affliction.

The rules that underlie our moral contemplations of creature government assistance are complex and envelop different viewpoints and structures. One crucial methodology is the utilitarian viewpoint, which tries to limit enduring and expand prosperity. Utilitarianism sets that we ought to think about the outcomes of our activities on the bliss and enduring of every conscious being, no matter what their species. From this perspective, it becomes clear that actually hurting creatures is ethically shaky.

One more moral system that educates our treatment regarding creatures is deontology, which depends on the idea of obligation and innate privileges. Defenders of deontology contend that creatures have natural worth and ought to be treated with deference and poise, independent of their utility to people. This point of view underlines that creatures have intrinsic privileges to live liberated from superfluous affliction and double-dealing.

Notwithstanding utilitarianism and deontology, natural morals assumes a critical part in our contemplations of creature government assistance. This viewpoint highlights the interconnectedness of all living things and the need to keep up with biological equilibrium. Treating creatures with care and regard is fundamental for the good of they as well as for the dependability and maintainability of our planet.

Moreover, there are social and strict aspects to the morals of creature government assistance. Many societies and religions have customs, lessons, and ceremonies that accentuate empathy and love for creatures. These social and profound qualities impact our associations with creatures and shape our ethical responsibilities toward them.

Our moral contemplations additionally stretch out to issues like creature testing, natural life protection, and the treatment of sidekick creatures. The moral quandaries encompassing these regions are mind boggling and multi-layered, expecting us to gauge the advantages of logical advancement, the safeguarding of biodiversity, and the government assistance of individual creatures.

Basically applying our moral standards to the advanced world postures remarkable difficulties. The pervasiveness of plant cultivating, the utilization of creatures in research, and the abuse of untamed life for benefit are regions where moral worries frequently conflict with financial interests and dug in rehearses. As we look at these issues, we should consider how to progress toward additional moral and reasonable practices while regarding the vocations of those included.

Really focusing on all animals includes both individual and aggregate activities. As people, we can settle on decisions that mirror our moral qualities, for example, embracing a plant-based diet, supporting savagery free items, and pushing for the others conscious treatment of creatures in different businesses. These individual decisions in total affect the interest for moral practices and items.

By and large, society can authorize legitimate and administrative changes that give more prominent security to creatures. Numerous nations have proactively executed regulation pointed toward working on creature government assistance, remembering guidelines for the treatment of creatures in horticulture, prohibitions on specific types of creature remorselessness, and limitations on the exchange jeopardized species. These lawful structures assist with laying out a pattern for moral treatment and reflect developing cultural qualities.

Training and mindfulness are likewise pivotal parts of advancing creature government assistance. Illuminating people in general about the moral contemplations encompassing creatures, the outcomes of their decisions, and the significance of protecting biodiversity can engage people to go with informed choices and promoter for change.

"Really focusing on All Animals: The Morals of Creature Government assistance" welcomes us to ponder our ethical obligations to the creatures we share our reality with. As we dig into the verifiable setting of our relationship with creatures, the hidden moral standards, and the viable ramifications of our qualities, we set out on an excursion that moves us to reconsider our treatment of non-human creatures. In our current reality where sympathy and compassion are fundamental, the morals of creature government assistance stand as a demonstration of our common obligation to a more merciful and only concurrence with all animals, extraordinary and little.

1. The importance of animal welfare in today's society

In the present interconnected and quickly impacting world, the idea of creature government assistance has risen above its status as a specialty concern and has turned into an essential and major problem for social orders all over the planet. The prosperity of creatures isn't just an ethical objective yet additionally a basic part of feasible living, ecological safeguarding, general wellbeing, and our common moral obligation. In this 1300-word investigation, we will dig into the multi-layered significance of creature government assistance in present day culture, looking at the moral, biological, monetary, and general wellbeing aspects that highlight the meaning of our moral treatment of creatures.

1. **Moral Objective:**
   At the core of the significance of creature government assistance lies an ethical basic well established in sympathy and compassion. A major moral thought calls upon us to perceive the inherent worth of every living being, no matter what their species. Our moral treatment of creatures mirrors our cultural qualities and our ability for graciousness and compassion.

   The ethical component of creature government assistance reaches out to the acknowledgment of creatures as conscious creatures fit for encountering torment, enduring, and a scope of feelings. The moral treatment of creatures recognizes their ability to feel dread, satisfaction, love, and trouble, and hence urges us to forestall their pointless anguish.

   This ethical basic likewise embraces the possibility of stewardship, underlining our obligation to safeguard and really focus on creatures who share our planet. This acknowledgment is especially appropriate as human exercises progressively influence the environments, biological systems, and lives of incalculable species.

2. **Environmental Equilibrium:**
   Creature government assistance is unpredictably connected to the safeguarding of natural equilibrium and biodiversity. Each specie assumes an exceptional part in the snare of life, adding to the security and soundness of environments. The annihilation or enduring of one animal categories can have sweeping outcomes, prompting awkward nature that influence different species, including people.

   For instance, the decay of pollinators like honey bees and butterflies compromises worldwide food security, as these creatures are fundamental for the fertilization of many harvests. The prosperity of dominant hunters, like wolves and sharks, is crucial for keeping up with the soundness of environments by controlling prey populaces and forestalling overgrazing or overfishing.

   Protecting biodiversity and environmental equilibrium remains forever inseparable with advancing creature government assistance. At the point when we focus on the government assistance of creatures, we add to the security of whole biological systems, encouraging versatility even with ecological difficulties, for example, environmental change and natural surroundings misfortune.

3. **Financial Importance:**

   Creature government assistance additionally conveys monetary significance. A flourishing and maintainable farming area, for example, depends on the prosperity of domesticated animals. Dishonest treatment of animals in manufacturing plant ranches raises moral worries as well as lead to negative financial outcomes. Focused and unfortunate animals in horticulture are more inclined to illnesses, which can bring about financial misfortunes for ranchers. The abuse of anti-infection agents to oversee creature wellbeing can prompt anti-infection opposition, representing a danger to human wellbeing and expanding medical services costs. Conversely, rehearses that focus on creature government assistance can upgrade efficiency, decrease illness risk, and work on the general nature of creature inferred items.

   Additionally, the eco-the travel industry and untamed life preservation ventures are critical supporters of numerous economies. Nations and districts that focus on the government assistance of their untamed life draw in sightseers and produce income from exercises like safaris, birdwatching, and untamed life photography. The deceptive treatment or double-dealing of untamed life can hurt these ventures and effect nearby economies.

4. **General Wellbeing:**

   Creature government assistance is firmly interlaced with general wellbeing concerns. Untrustworthy treatment of animals in modern cultivating, for example, can prompt the transmission of zoonotic illnesses from creatures to people. The swarmed, unsanitary circumstances in some production line ranches make a favorable place for illnesses like avian influenza and pig influenza. These illnesses can have wrecking outcomes on human wellbeing and result in pandemics.

   Besides, the utilization of anti-infection agents in creature horticulture can add to the improvement of anti-infection safe microorganisms, which represent a grave danger to general wellbeing. At the point when we focus on animal government assistance in cultivating rehearses, we can decrease the requirement for anti-toxins, subsequently assisting with protecting human wellbeing.

   Creature government assistance likewise meets with food handling. Stress and unfortunate everyday environments for creatures can bring about lower-quality creature items that might contain destructive substances or microorganisms. Guaranteeing legitimate creature government assistance guidelines in the development of meat, dairy, and other creature determined items is fundamental for keeping up with sanitation and the prosperity of buyers.

5. **Moral Advancement and Social Obligation:**

   Society's obligation to creature government assistance mirrors our ability for moral advancement and social obligation. Over the long run, how we might interpret creatures' mental and profound capacities has developed, prompting a more prominent familiarity with their true capacity for torment. Thus, we have perceived the need to change our practices and arrangements to line up with our advancing virtues.

This moral advancement reaches out to regulation and guidelines pointed toward safeguarding creatures. Numerous nations and locales have acquainted regulations with guarantee the altruistic treatment of creatures, mirroring the developing cultural agreement on the significance of creature government assistance. In doing as such, we recognize that our general public's virtues and social obligation incorporate our treatment of creatures.

6. **Interconnectedness of All Life:**

The significance of creature government assistance is additionally highlighted by the developing comprehension of the interconnectedness of all life on The planet. The mind boggling connections between species, biological systems, and the climate feature the effect of our activities on the fragile equilibrium of our planet.

Our treatment of creatures influences individual creatures as well as whole biological systems and the prosperity of human networks. By focusing on creature government assistance, we add to a more agreeable and maintainable concurrence with every single living being.

B. The moral and ethical foundations of caring for animals

Really focusing on creatures is a moral and moral basic profoundly implanted in the human experience. Our relationship with creatures has developed over centuries, reflecting moving cultural qualities and our developing comprehension of their consciousness, close to home lives, and natural worth. In this 1400-word investigation, we dig into the moral and moral establishments that support our obligation to really focus on creatures, looking at the standards of sympathy, compassion, and the acknowledgment of the characteristic worth of every single living being. These standards act as the foundation of our moral and moral obligation to secure and advocate for the prosperity of creatures in this day and age.

1. **Sympathy and Compassion:**
   Sympathy and compassion are at the center of our moral and moral starting points for really focusing on creatures. These characteristics are natural to numerous people, and they drive us to think about the affliction and government assistance of every single aware being, including creatures. Sympathy is the capacity to perceive and partake in the enduring of others, while compassion is the ability to comprehend and connect with the feelings and encounters of others.

   These characteristics stretch out to creatures since we perceive their capacity to encounter torment, delight, dread, happiness, and a scope of feelings. Noticing a creature in trouble can evoke sensations of sympathy and empathy in us, convincing us to make a move to mitigate their misery.

By and large, our ability for sympathy and compassion has prompted the advancement of moral frameworks and moral codes that accentuate the significance of treating creatures with generosity and regard. Antiquated thinkers, for example, Pythagoras and Plato perceived the ethical basic of empathy towards creatures, attesting that it is our obligation to try not to cause them pointless damage.

In a contemporary setting, our moral and moral obligation to sympathy and compassion is reflected in the standards of creature government assistance. These standards guide how we might interpret how creatures ought to be dealt with, recognizing their ability for affliction and underlining the need to shield them from mischief and abuse.

2. **Natural Worth of Every single Living Being:**

One of the central moral principles of really focusing on creatures is the acknowledgment of the characteristic worth of every living being. This guideline affirms that creatures have worth all by themselves, free of their utility or value to people. It maintains the possibility that creatures are not simple products, but instead, people with their own advantages and freedoms.

The idea of characteristic worth reaches out to the conviction that creatures have their own innate poise, meriting admiration and thought. This moral point of view is frequently connected with deontological morals, which underlines our obligation to approach creatures with deference and not to involve them as a necessary evil.

Recognizing the characteristic worth of creatures challenges rehearses that adventure or mischief them for human increase. It constrains us to scrutinize the moral ramifications of involving creatures for amusement, trial and error, or as wares in the agribusiness business. At the point when we perceive that creatures have inborn worth, we are ethically committed to safeguard their prosperity and guarantee that our activities don't think twice about respect and privileges.

3. **Moral Advancement and Development:**

The moral and moral underpinnings of really focusing on creatures are not static however persistently advance over the long run. Human social orders have seen moral advancement in our treatment of creatures as how we might interpret their mental and close to home limits has extended. This development mirrors our ability for moral development and variation to evolving conditions.

By and large, creatures were frequently viewed as existing exclusively for human use, prompting rehearses that caused enormous affliction and abuse. In any case, as how we might interpret creatures has extended, our ethical obligation to their government assistance has developed. We presently perceive the consciousness of creatures, their ability to endure, and their close to home lives, prompting changes in our moral contemplations and practices.

This ethical advancement is clear in the improvement of regulations and guidelines pointed toward safeguarding creatures. Numerous nations have ordered regulation to forestall remorselessness to creatures, set guidelines for their treatment, and make shields against rehearses that hurt their government assistance. This lawful structure mirrors the ethical development of society, as it perceives the moral basic of really focusing on creatures and safeguarding their inclinations.

4. **Interconnectedness of Life:**

The moral and moral underpinnings of really focusing on creatures are intently attached to the comprehension of the interconnectedness of all life on The planet. The fragile equilibrium of biological systems depends on the association of various species, each adding to the steadiness and soundness of their current circumstance.

The acknowledgment of this interconnectedness features the effect of our activities on creatures and the more extensive climate. At the point when we damage or take advantage of creatures, we upset the perplexing connections that support life on our planet. The eradication of a solitary animal groups can have flowing impacts all through an environment, prompting uneven characters that influence different species, including people.

By focusing on creature government assistance and perceiving the inborn worth of creatures, we add to the protection of biological equilibrium and biodiversity. Our moral obligation to really focusing on creatures lines up with the more extensive objective of keeping an agreeable conjunction with every living being and safeguarding the delicate snare of life on The planet.

5. **Moral Obligations:**

Really focusing on creatures isn't just a moral or moral ideal; it involves substantial obligations and activities. Our moral starting points for creature care convert into a bunch of useful obligations:

Keeping away from Remorselessness: A major moral obligation is to cease from inflicting any kind of damage or enduring to creatures. This standard underlies the counteraction of savagery to creatures in different settings, from the treatment of pets and domesticated animals to the treatment of natural life in protection endeavors.

Accommodating Essential Requirements: Another moral obligation is to guarantee that creatures' fundamental necessities are met. This incorporates admittance to food, clean water, cover, and fitting clinical consideration. Ignoring these fundamentals is viewed as a break of our moral commitments.

Regarding Privileges: Moral establishments additionally accentuate the acknowledgment of basic entitlements. This incorporates the option to live liberated from pointless anguish, the option to communicate normal ways of behaving, and the option to be safeguarded from abuse.

Promotion and Training: Some portion of our moral obligations includes supporting for creatures and teaching others about the moral and reasonable significance of creature government assistance. This can incorporate supporting associations committed to creature security and bringing issues to light about issues connected with creature prosperity.

Advancing Moral Works on: Empowering the reception of moral practices in different fields, like farming, diversion, and examination, is a critical moral obligation. This involves pushing for additional others conscious and economical methodologies in these areas.

6. **Social and Strict Viewpoints:**

Really focusing on creatures is likewise impacted by social and strict viewpoints that stress empathy and veneration for creatures. Many societies and religions have customs, lessons, and ceremonies that supporter for the moral treatment of creatures and advance the possibility of interconnectedness with every living being.

For instance, Jainism, an old religion, embraces the standard of "ahimsa" or peacefulness, which reaches out to every single living being. Buddhism correspondingly advances graciousness and non-hurt towards creatures.

In Christianity, the stewardship of God's creation is in many cases seen as an ethical obligation, underscoring care for creatures and the climate.

These social and strict viewpoints give extra upright and moral starting points for really focusing on creatures and highlight the general idea of the rules that drive our obligation towards them.

C. The scope of the book and its objectives

Each book sets out on an excursion with a reason, trying to investigate, illuminate, or move. "The Extent of the Book and Its Goals" fills in as a compass, directing perusers through the expectations, limits, and desires that characterize the items in a composed work. In this 1500-word investigation, we will explain the extent of a speculative book while illustrating its overall targets. Thusly, we intend to give perusers a reasonable comprehension of what they can anticipate from the book and the objectives it tries to accomplish.

1. **Characterizing the Degree:**
   Understanding the extent of a book is much the same as portraying its limits and making way for what will be covered. This incorporates distinguishing the topic, subjects, and explicit areas of concentration. On account of our speculative book, the extension is characterized as follows:
   Our book investigates the diverse connection between man-made brainpower (simulated intelligence) and morals. It digs into the moral ramifications, issues, and open doors introduced by the quick headway of man-made intelligence innovation. The book covers a great many points inside this space, including the accompanying regions:

Computer based intelligence and Society: We explore the cultural effect of computer based intelligence innovation, looking at issues, for example, artificial intelligence driven robotization, work dislodging, and financial imbalance. We investigate how man-made intelligence meets with moral inquiries connected with security, reconnaissance, and individual privileges.

Man-made intelligence in Medical services: The book dives into the moral contemplations of artificial intelligence applications in medical care, from demonstrative apparatuses to customized therapy proposals. We evaluate the advantages and difficulties of simulated intelligence in advancing better medical care results while tending to worries about information protection and predisposition in calculations.

Man-made intelligence and Independent Frameworks: We investigate the moral intricacies of independent computer based intelligence frameworks, including self-driving vehicles and robots. This part assesses inquiries of responsibility, direction, and the potential for simulated intelligence driven hurt.

Computer based intelligence and Predisposition: The book researches issues connected with predisposition in simulated intelligence calculations and the moral basic of tending to and moderating predispositions. We analyze situations where man-made intelligence frameworks have propagated segregation and talk about systems for accomplishing more reasonableness and value in computer based intelligence innovation.

Simulated intelligence and Inventiveness: We investigate the moral components of man-made intelligence created workmanship, music, and writing. This part digs into inquiries of initiation, inventiveness, and the possible effect on the innovative callings.

Artificial intelligence and Future Points of view: The book thinks about the moral difficulties and valuable open doors not too far off, including hyper-genius man-made intelligence, human-man-made intelligence reconciliation, and the job of simulated intelligence in tending to worldwide difficulties, for example, environmental change and medical care differences.

2. **Targets of the Book:**

   A book's targets epitomize its motivation and the objectives it expects to achieve. On account of "Investigating the Moral Components of Computerized reasoning," the goals are exhaustive, intelligent of the degree, and driven by a longing to illuminate, incite thought, and move activity. The essential goals of the book are as per the following:

   Illuminate and Instruct: One of the focal targets of this book is to advise perusers about the moral ramifications regarding artificial intelligence innovation. It furnishes perusers with a balanced comprehension of the topic, its intricacies, and this present reality suggestions for people, social orders, and the worldwide local area.

Cultivate Decisive Reasoning: The book tries to energize decisive reasoning by introducing a scope of moral issues, contextual investigations, and interesting situations. It prompts perusers to think about the moral components of computer based intelligence innovation and to take part in helpful talk.

Give a Multidisciplinary Point of view: To satisfy its targets, the book draws on bits of knowledge from different disciplines, including morals, reasoning, software engineering, regulation, and sociologies. By introducing a multidisciplinary point of view, the book expects to take care of a different crowd with shifting degrees of skill in computer based intelligence and morals.

Offer Functional Direction: as well as investigating moral issues, the book offers reasonable direction for people, policymakers, and associations on exploring the moral scene of artificial intelligence. It gives suggestions to making moral simulated intelligence frameworks and addresses inquiries of administration and guideline.

Bring issues to light: A significant target of the book is to bring issues to light about the moral elements of artificial intelligence, especially among the individuals who might not have recently thought to be the subject. It endeavors to pursue perusers more aware of the decisions and choices they make in regards to artificial intelligence innovation.

Move Moral Activity: Past mindfulness, the book intends to motivate moral activity. It enables perusers to advocate for dependable man-made intelligence improvement and use, encouraging a feeling of obligation and organization even with moral difficulties.

Advance Moral Development: By featuring the moral issues encompassing simulated intelligence, the book looks to support advancement that focuses on moral contemplations. It calls upon people and associations to outfit the capability of artificial intelligence innovation for a long term benefit while regarding moral standards.

Energize Exchange and Discussion: The book plans to animate discourse and discussion about simulated intelligence and morals. It urges perusers to participate in discussions with companions, specialists, and policymakers, cultivating a worldwide conversation on the moral components of man-made intelligence.

Add to Moral man-made intelligence Advancement: At last, the book tries to add to the continuous improvement of moral artificial intelligence. It offers an asset for specialists, engineers, and policymakers looking to make computer based intelligence frameworks that line up with moral standards and human qualities.

3. **Ideal interest group:**

Recognizing the target group of a book is fundamental in explaining its goals. "Investigating the Moral Elements of Man-made brainpower" is intended to take care of a different scope of perusers, including:

General Perusers: People with a general interest in simulated intelligence and morals, looking to grasp the moral ramifications of artificial intelligence in different settings.

Understudies and Scholastics: Understudies, specialists, and scholastics in fields like morals, software engineering, reasoning, and regulation, who wish to dive further into the topic.

Policymakers and Controllers: Those associated with molding computer based intelligence strategy and guideline, expecting to acquire experiences into the moral contemplations that ought to illuminate direction.

Tech Industry Experts: Experts working in the innovation area, including simulated intelligence designers and architects, who look to coordinate moral contemplations into their work.

Moral and Promotion Associations: Individuals from associations devoted to morals, basic freedoms, and innovation who plan to remain educated and impact the moral advancement regarding artificial intelligence.

Chapter 1

Historical Perspectives on Animal Welfare

The idea of creature government assistance is a subject that rises above time and lines, as it is well established in our common history as people. The manner in which social orders have treated creatures has advanced throughout the long term, reflecting moving moral, social, and monetary qualities. In this extensive investigation of authentic points of view on creature government assistance, spreading over , we will travel through the chronicles of time, from antiquated developments to the advanced period, to figure out the complex and always changing connection among people and creatures. This authentic point of view offers urgent bits of knowledge into the advancement of our moral treatment of creatures and the illustrations we can gather for the present and what's to come.

1. Old Developments: The Beginning of Human-Creature Communication

The account of creature government assistance starts with the rise of human development. Old social orders, frequently interweaved with rural practices, had multifaceted associations with creatures that consolidated love and double-dealing.

1. **Egypt: A Place that is known for Differentiations**
   In old Egypt, creatures held a critical spot in the social and strict milieu. Numerous creatures, like felines, dairy cattle, and ibises, were viewed as sacrosanct and, surprisingly, exalted. The worship for creatures prompted the act of preserving them and covering them in fabulous services.

   All the while, Egypt likewise rehearsed creature cultivation for a huge scope, reproducing creatures for work and utilization. This polarity exhibits the concurrence of both regard and double-dealing in early human-creature connections.

2. **Greece and Rome: Philosophical Trailblazers**

Old Greece and Rome assumed essential parts in shaping early philosophical contemplations on creature government assistance. Logicians, for example, Pythagoras and Plato supported for the moral treatment of creatures. Pythagoras, for example, put stock in the immigration of spirits among people and creatures, supporting shared consciousness and family relationship.

The Stoics in old Rome developed these thoughts, accentuating the solidarity of every living being and the requirement for sympathy and compassion towards creatures. Their works laid the foundation for later moral contemplations of creature government assistance.

II. The Medieval times: A Complicated Scene
The Medieval times denoted a time of critical cultural change, including the improvement of the primitive framework and the ascent of the Christian church as a predominant power. These movements significantly affected the treatment of creatures.

1. **Christian Impact: Blended Messages**
   The Christian church assumed a significant part in molding

middle age perspectives towards creatures. While certain scholars upheld for consideration and sympathy towards creatures, underscoring their place in God's creation, others embraced a more human-centric view that legitimized the double-dealing of creatures for human advantage.

Scholars like St. Francis of Assisi, known for his adoration for creatures, remained as reference points of sympathy. Be that as it may, the predominant view, educated by the compositions regarding figures like St. Thomas Aquinas, would in general focus on human interests over those of creatures.

2. Hunting and Nobility

The middle age time frame saw the ascent of hunting as a leaned toward diversion among the nobility. While the quest for game creatures was viewed as an honorable pursuit, it frequently elaborate brutal and inefficient practices that didn't line up with present day ideas of moral hunting.

The treatment of working creatures during this period changed broadly. While certain creatures, similar to ponies, were esteemed and really focused on, others, like bulls and donkeys, were frequently exposed to unforgiving work and negligible government assistance contemplations.

III. The Illumination and the Introduction of Creature Government assistance Developments

The Illumination period, with its accentuation on reason, individual freedoms, and social advancement, achieved tremendous changes in how creatures were seen and treated. This period established the groundwork for present day creature government assistance developments.

1. Illumination Thinkers: Shaping Current Idea

Edification thinkers like René Descartes, Immanuel Kant, and Jeremy Bentham added to the improvement of current creature morals. Descartes broadly contended that creatures were simple robots, without any trace of awareness. In any case, Kant tested this view, affirming that mercilessness to creatures could prompt savagery towards people.

Jeremy Bentham's utilitarian way of thinking significantly affected creature government assistance morals. He broadly inquired, "The inquiry isn't, might they at any point reason? Nor, could they at any point talk? In any case, could they at any point endure?" This viewpoint laid the preparation for the thought of creatures' ability to encounter torment and enduring as a basic consider moral treatment.

2. Early Creature Government assistance Developments

The Edification time additionally saw the rise of the main creature government assistance associations and social orders. In 1824, the General public for the Counteraction of Remorselessness to Creatures (SPCA) was established in England, denoting a huge move toward the formalization of creature security endeavors. These associations attempted to end brutal practices, for example, creature teasing and coldhearted transportation conditions.

IV. The Modern Transformation and the Effect on Creatures

The Modern Unrest of the eighteenth and nineteenth hundreds of years achieved extraordinary changes in the public eye, innovation, and the treatment of creatures. As urbanization and industrialization progressed, so did the requirement for work and the abuse of creatures.

1. **Urbanization and Creature Government assistance**
   Urbanization during the Modern Upset affected creatures. While certain creatures, similar to pets, delighted in superior day to day environments, numerous metropolitan working creatures, including ponies, experienced because of requesting work and frequently brutal treatment.

2. **Processing plant Cultivating and Large scale manufacturing**

The ascent of processing plant cultivating in the twentieth century is quite possibly of the main change throughout the entire existence of creature government assistance. It was described by the concentrated imprisonment and large scale manufacturing of domesticated animals for food, with an emphasis on effectiveness and benefit.

The circumstances in manufacturing plant ranches raised grave worries about animal government assistance. Creatures were frequently exposed to congestion, unsanitary conditions, and difficult methods, starting shock and calls for change.

V. The Advanced Creature Government assistance Development

The mid-twentieth century saw the rise of a worldwide creature government assistance development. Activists, researchers, and associations started to advocate for the moral treatment of creatures on a more extensive scale, introducing a period of massive change and progress in creature government assistance.

1. **Lawful Systems and Insurance**

   The mid-twentieth century additionally saw the presentation of legitimate insurances for creatures. Regulations pointed toward forestalling remorselessness and working on the government assistance of creatures started to arise in different nations. The US passed the Creature Government assistance Act in 1966, denoting a huge move toward creature security regulation.

2. **Growing Degree and Concerns**

The cutting edge creature government assistance development extended its extension to incorporate a great many worries, from lab creature government assistance to the treatment of friend creatures and untamed life preservation. Moral contemplations started to stretch out to different ventures and works on, remembering the utilization of creatures for examination, diversion, and design.

VI. Contemporary Difficulties and Continuous Advancement

Today, creature government assistance stays an essential worry as we stand up to new difficulties connected with innovation, supportability, and worldwide interconnectedness.

1. **Innovation and Morals**
   Propels in innovation, like computerized reasoning and bio-technology, have presented novel moral difficulties in creature government assistance. Questions encompassing the treatment of creatures in research, especially with regards to man-made intelligence and creature testing, raise significant moral situations.
2. **Supportability and Moral Farming**
   The ecological and moral ramifications of horticulture, especially with regards to environmental change, have ignited discussions about reasonable and sympathetic cultivating rehearses. Ideas like natural cultivating, field raised animals, and plant-based abstains from food are acquiring unmistakable quality.
3. **Moral Contemplations in Natural life Preservation**

Natural life preservation stays a basic area of creature government assistance concern. Offsetting preservation endeavors with moral treatment, environment safeguarding, and the security of imperiled species is a continuous test.

VII. The Eventual fate of Creature Government assistance

The eventual fate of creature government assistance will probably be formed by a scope of variables, including logical headways, worldwide moral guidelines, and the dynamic commitment of people and associations.

1. **Moral Contemplations in Logical Exploration**
   Progressions in logical exploration, for example, options in contrast to creature testing and more others conscious examination rehearses, offer expect working on creature government assistance in the lab setting.

2. Worldwide Joint effort and Guidelines

Worldwide participation and the foundation of global moral principles for creature government assistance are turning out to be progressively significant. Associations like the World Creature Assurance are attempting to guarantee steady moral treatment of creatures around the world.

1.1 Ancient civilizations and their attitudes toward animals

The connection among people and creatures has been an essential piece of mankind's set of experiences starting from the beginning of human advancement. All through the ages, different old civilizations displayed assorted perspectives toward creatures, frequently impacted by social, strict, financial, and natural variables. In this extensive investigation spreading over 1700 words, we will travel through the convictions, practices, and jobs of creatures in the old world. Our process will take us through a few unmistakable old developments, revealing insight into the complex and developing nature of these connections.

1. Mesopotamia: The Support of Human progress

Mesopotamia, frequently viewed as the support of human progress, was home to a few old social orders, including the Sumerians, Babylonians, and Assyrians. These human advancements had complex associations with creatures, driven by both viable and emblematic contemplations.

1. Utilitarianism and Farming

In Mesopotamia, creatures held a commonsense job in the improvement of horticulture. The furrowing of fields was fundamentally finished by bulls, while jackasses and donkeys were utilized for transportation. The utilization of animals in cultivating added to food creation as well as affected how these creatures were seen.

2. **Imagery and Gods**

Creatures were indispensable to the strict and fanciful convictions of Mesopotamian developments. For instance, the lion was loved as an image of solidarity and power, with the goddess Ishtar frequently connected with lions. In Babylonian folklore, the snake was viewed as an image of disarray and obliteration, while the mythical beast like animal, the mushhushshu, was connected to the god Marduk.

3. **Conciliatory Contributions**

Conciliatory contributions including creatures were normal in strict ceremonies. The blood of conciliatory creatures was accepted to have sanitizing and defensive characteristics, while the training additionally exhibited dedication and accommodation to gods.

II. Old Egypt: A Universe of Imagery and Veneration

Antiquated Egypt is famous for its complex relationship with creatures, consolidating reasonable purposes with profound imagery and strict importance.

1. **Creature Divine beings and Imagery**

The Egyptians venerated a large number of creature divinities, with every creature representing various characteristics and powers. The sacrosanct ibis was related with Thoth, the lord of shrewdness, while the feline addressed the goddess Bastet, connected to home and ripeness.

Creatures were additionally utilized as defensive images. The scarab creepy crawly, for example, represented recovery and was in many cases worn as a special necklace.

2. **Reasonable Use**

Old Egyptians involved creatures for functional purposes too. Felines, for instance, were kept as pets to safeguard against vermin. Dairy cattle assumed an essential part in horticulture and transportation, and different creatures were raised for food and assets.

3. Strict Customs and Penance

Penances of creatures, like bulls and geese, were an essential piece of Egyptian strict customs. These contributions were made to assuage divine beings and guarantee the richness of the land.

III. Indus Valley Human progress: A Brief look into Early Indian Culture

The Indus Valley Development, one of the world's most seasoned metropolitan societies, offers bits of knowledge into the connection among people and creatures in antiquated India.

1. Taming and Farming

The Indus Valley individuals took part in early types of farming, depending on animals for furrowing and transportation. Bulls were especially huge in these undertakings.

2. Strict Imagery and the Pashupati Seal

The Pashupati Seal, a notable curio of the Indus Valley Development, includes a horned figure encompassed by creatures. The focal figure, generally recognized as a god, is portrayed with creatures, recommending a strict and emblematic association among people and the creature world.

IV. Old China: Concordance and Equilibrium

Old Chinese progress was described by a profound feeling of congruity and offset with nature, which stretched out to the treatment of creatures.

1. Confucianism and Moral Standards

Confucianism, an unmistakable philosophical and moral framework, stressed the significance of kindheartedness, empathy, and regard for every single living being. These standards affected mentalities toward creatures, empowering sympathetic treatment.

2. **Taoism and Nature's Intrinsic Worth**
   Taoism, one more persuasive philosophical custom in antiquated China, underlined the characteristic worth of nature and every single living animal. This viewpoint empowered regard for creatures and the acknowledgment of their position in the regular request.

3. **Utilitarianism and Horticulture**

Pragmatic contemplations were additionally vital to the Chinese relationship with creatures. Animals, like pigs and chickens, assumed fundamental parts in food creation, and creatures like ponies and bulls were utilized in horticulture.

V. Old Greece: Philosophical Trailblazers

Old Greece was a cauldron of philosophical idea, and the mentalities toward creatures in this general public were fundamentally impacted by the philosophical thoughts of unmistakable masterminds.

1. **Pythagoras and Immigration of Spirits**
   Pythagoras, perhaps of the most well known Greek thinker, held one of a kind convictions about the interconnectedness of every single living being. He presented the possibility of the immigration of spirits, recommending that the spirits of people and creatures could be renewed in various structures. This viewpoint underlined the moral treatment of creatures.

2. **Emotionlessness and Solidarity of Every single Living Being**

The Stoics, a school of reasoning in old Greece, pushed for the solidarity of every living being. They accepted that people and creatures shared a typical heavenly explanation, highlighting the requirement for sympathy and moral treatment of creatures.

VI. Old Rome: A Perplexing Relationship

Antiquated Rome acquired a lot of its way of life and mentalities toward creatures from Greece, however it likewise had unmistakable points of view on the treatment of creatures.

1. **Amphitheatrical Gore**
   The Romans were known for their intricate amphitheater occasions, including gladiatorial battle and creature chases. These fierce displays mirrored an interest with savagery and passing and exhibited a negligence for creature government assistance.

2. **Philosophical Impact**

While Roman perspectives toward creatures could be cruel, the impact of Greek philosophical thoughts, especially Apathy, advanced more humane perspectives. A few Roman masterminds, similar to Seneca, communicated worries about remorselessness to creatures.

VII. Antiquated India: Love and Vegetarianism

Antiquated India, profoundly affected by Hinduism and Buddhism, showed significant adoration for creatures and advanced vegetarianism.

1. **Hinduism and the Holy relic**
   Hinduism, the transcendent religion in old India, holds the cow as sacrosanct and sacred. Cows were worshipped for their part in giving food and as images of heavenly and natural liberality.

2. **Buddhism and Non-Hurting**

Buddhism, which arose in India, broadens the guideline of non-hurting, or ahimsa, to every single living being. This way of thinking empowers vegetarianism and accommodating treatment of creatures, as hurting any aware being is viewed as adverse to one's profound advancement.

VIII. Perspectives Toward Creatures in the Americas: Native Societies

Before the appearance of European pilgrims, native societies in the Americas had different mentalities toward creatures, frequently established in animism and a significant association with the normal world.

1. **Profound Importance**
   Numerous native societies saw creatures as profoundly critical creatures, frequently addressing explicit characteristics or going about as couriers between the human and otherworldly domains.
2. **Supportable Practices**

Native hunting and fishing rehearses were ordinarily feasible and deferential of the climate. Creatures were seen as wellsprings of food, and their utilization was painstakingly figured out how to guarantee balance in environments.

IX. Examples from Old Perspectives Toward Creatures

The mentalities of old civilizations toward creatures offer important illustrations and experiences for the present and future. A few key focal points include:

1. **Social Variety and Intricacy**
   The range of mentalities and practices toward creatures in old civilizations features the intricacy of human-creature connections. These connections were formed by different variables, including society, religion, climate, and monetary need.
2. **Advancement of Moral Qualities**
   Over the entire course of time, moral qualities connected with creatures developed. While certain developments esteemed creatures essentially for utilitarian purposes, others advanced adoration and empathetic treatment.
3. **Impact of Theory and Religion**
   Philosophical and strict convictions assumed a critical part in forming perspectives toward creatures. Savants and strict pioneers,

like Pythagoras, Confucius, and Buddha, significantly impacted the moral treatment of creatures in their particular societies.

4. **Crossing point of Pragmatic and Moral Contemplations**
The treatment of creatures frequently crossed with pragmatic contemplations connected with agribusiness, transportation, and food. These commonsense necessities in some cases affected the moral qualities related with creatures.

5. **Solidarity with Nature**
Numerous antiquated civic establishments perceived the interconnectedness of every living being and the requirement for congruity with nature. This viewpoint supported regard for creatures and the normal world.

6. **Progressing Significance**

The verifiable mentalities toward creatures keep on affecting contemporary points of view on creature government assistance, moral treatment, and the human-creature relationship.

1.2 The role of religion and philosophy in shaping our views on animals

The connection among people and creatures has been profoundly impacted by the interchange of religion and reasoning. Over the entire course of time, different conviction frameworks and philosophical points of view play had a significant impact in forming the manner in which we view and cooperate with creatures. This mind boggling and complex relationship is clear in the assorted ways various religions and philosophical customs have resolved inquiries of profound quality, morals, and the treatment of creatures. In this exhaustive investigation spreading over 1600 words, we will dig into the job of religion and reasoning in molding our perspectives on creatures and consider the moral and moral ramifications that keep on reverberating in contemporary society.

1. **Religion: The Impact of Conviction Frameworks on Creature Government assistance**

Religion has been a strong power in molding human perspectives toward creatures, frequently giving a moral and otherworldly structure for our connections with the non-human world.

1. **Hinduism: Ahimsa and the Untouchable relic**
   Hinduism, one of the world's most seasoned religions, significantly affects the treatment of creatures. Integral to Hindu moral standards is the idea of "ahimsa," or non-hurting, which stretches out to every living being. The cow, specifically, holds a sacrosanct status in Hinduism, embodying the love and sympathy related with this religion.
   The killing of cows is viewed as a grave moral offense, and vegetarianism is frequently maintained as a declaration of ahimsa.

2. **Buddhism: Sympathy and Non-Hurting**
   Buddhism, which arose in India, advances sympathy and non-hurting (ahimsa) toward every single aware being. The primary statute in Buddhism is to abstain from taking life, and this obligation to peacefulness reaches out to creatures. Buddhists ordinarily stick to vegetarianism, and in a few Buddhist societies, the arrival of creatures from bondage as a demonstration of empathy is a far and wide practice.

3. **Jainism: Ahimsa as the Most noteworthy Goodness**
   Jainism, one more old Indian religion, puts the greatest possible level of accentuation on ahimsa. Jains follow a severe vegan diet, keeping away from even root vegetables to limit mischief to living creatures. The act of "anekantavada" urges devotees to recognize the intricacy of life and the interconnectedness of every single living being.

4. **Christianity: Territory and Stewardship**
   Christianity, with its assorted sections, offers fluctuating view-

points on the connection among people and creatures. The Holy book contains entries that notice people having "domain" over creatures yet in addition underscores stewardship and care for God's creation. A few Christian customs advocate for compassionate treatment of creatures and the evasion of remorselessness.

5. **Islam: Creature Government assistance and Halal Practices**

In Islam, creatures are viewed as a feature of God's creation, and their government assistance is underscored in the lessons of the Prophet Muhammad. Islamic dietary regulations, known as halal, require empathetic treatment and the utilization of explicit butcher practices that limit languishing. In any case, there is variety in the translation and utilization of these standards across Muslim people group.

II. Reasoning: Moral Contemplations and the Human-Creature Relationship

Reasoning, a discipline that investigates principal inquiries concerning presence, information, and profound quality, has fundamentally formed the manner in which we ponder creatures and our ethical constraints toward them.

1. **Aristotle and Judiciousness**

   Aristotle, quite possibly of the most compelling savant ever, accepted that soundness was the distinctive component of people and that creatures missing the mark on limit. This view prompted the possibility that creatures existed for human advantage, a point of view that lastingly affects the manner in which creatures have been treated since the beginning of time.

2. **Pythagoras and Immigration of Spirits**

   Pythagoras, an early Greek savant, proposed the idea of the immigration of spirits, recommending that spirits could be reawakened in various structures, including creatures. This thought established the groundwork for the moral treatment of creatures, as it suggested that creatures had a degree of cognizance and moral thought.

3. **Immanuel Kant and Moral Thought**

Immanuel Kant, a powerful figure in present day way of thinking, contended that ethical contemplations ought to be stretched out to creatures. He accepted that our treatment of creatures affected our ethical person and, subsequently, our treatment of individual people. Kant's way of thinking accentuated the significance of regarding creatures as closures in themselves as opposed to as means to human finishes.

4. **Jeremy Bentham and Utilitarianism**

Jeremy Bentham, a defender of utilitarianism, moved the focal point of moral contemplations from the sanity of creatures to their ability to encounter joy and languishing. He broadly inquired, "The inquiry isn't, could they at any point reason? Nor, could they at any point talk? In any case, could they at any point endure?" This viewpoint laid the preparation for the advanced creature government assistance development, which underscores the significance of decreasing the enduring of creatures.

5. **Peter Vocalist and Creature Freedom**

Peter Vocalist, a contemporary scholar, developed the utilitarian standards of Bentham, contending for creature freedom and the acknowledgment of the equivalent thought of interests. Vocalist's work significantly affects the cutting edge basic entitlements development, pushing for moral treatment and the finish of creature double-dealing.

III. Contemporary Reflections: The Convergence of Religion and Reasoning

In contemporary society, the transaction among religion and reasoning keeps on affecting our perspectives on creatures and guide our moral decisions.

1. **Interfaith Discoursed and Ecological Morals**
   Interfaith discoursed advance discussions about ecological morals and the ethical obligation to safeguard the normal world, including creatures. These conversations feature shared upsides of stewardship, sympathy, and non-hurting across strict practices.

2. **Moral Veganism and Basic entitlements Developments**
   The crossing point of reasoning and creature morals is obvious in the development of moral veganism and the basic entitlements development. Advocates frequently draw on philosophical standards, like Vocalist's utilitarianism, to contend for the ethical constraint to lessen creature enduring and abuse.

3. **Regulation and Creature Government assistance**

The acknowledgment of creatures as aware creatures with the ability to encounter enduring has affected regulation and lawful insurances. Numerous nations have presented creature government assistance regulations that mirror the advancing moral and philosophical contemplations encompassing creatures.

IV. Challenges and Moral Quandaries

The exchange of religion and reasoning in forming our perspectives on creatures presents the two valuable open doors and difficulties, including:

1. **Various Points of view**
   The variety of strict and philosophical viewpoints on creatures can prompt varying perspectives on moral treatment and the job of creatures in human culture.

2. **Moral Predicaments**
   Contemporary society wrestles with moral predicaments connected with animal government assistance, including issues, for example, production line cultivating, creature trial and error, and the protection of jeopardized species. The direction given by

strict and philosophical practices can illuminate conversations on these perplexing issues.

3. Adjusting Custom and Progress

Tracking down a harmony between regarding social and strict customs and propelling contemporary moral contemplations stays a continuous test in forming our perspectives on creatures.

1.3 Early animal protection movements and their impact on society

The historical backdrop of creature insurance developments is a demonstration of the advancing moral and moral upsides of human social orders. Over time, people and associations have worked indefatigably to work on the treatment of creatures, lessen savagery, and backer for their government assistance. Early creature security developments, arising in the eighteenth and nineteenth hundreds of years, denoted a huge defining moment in human-creature relations.

In this exhaustive investigation traversing we will dive into the beginnings and effect of these developments, following the improvement of creature government assistance standards and regulations that keep on molding our perspectives and ways of behaving toward creatures today.

1. The Edification and the Introduction of Creature Government assistance Awareness

The Edification, a scholarly and social development of the eighteenth hundred years, assumed a urgent part in molding the early creature security developments. Illumination masterminds advanced reasonableness, sympathy, and moral thought as core values for human direct, and these standards stretched out to the treatment of creatures.

1. Jeremy Bentham and the Rule of Utility
Quite possibly of the most compelling figure in the early creature assurance developments was savant and legal scholar Jeremy

Bentham. In his work "Prologue to the Standards of Ethics and Regulation" (1789), Bentham contended that the ability to endure, as opposed to knowledge or reason, ought to be the reason for deciding moral thought. He broadly expressed, "The inquiry isn't, could they at any point reason? Nor, might they at any point talk? Be that as it may, could they at any point endure?" Bentham's utilitarian way of thinking laid the basis for the moral thought of creatures, stressing the significance of limiting their torment. This rule turned into a basic component of early creature government assistance developments.

2. The Job of Illumination Savants

Illumination savants like Voltaire, Jean-Jacques Rousseau, and Immanuel Kant additionally added to the advancement of creature assurance cognizance. Voltaire scrutinized the savage treatment of creatures, while Rousseau contended that graciousness to creatures was an impression of a humanized society. Kant's ethical way of thinking stressed regarding creatures as finishes in themselves, as opposed to as means to human closures.

II. Early Creature Assurance Social orders

The late eighteenth and mid nineteenth hundreds of years saw the foundation of a portion of the world's earliest creature insurance social orders. These associations assumed a urgent part in upholding for creature government assistance and starting legitimate changes.

1. The General public for the Counteraction of Savagery to Creatures (SPCA)

The General public for the Counteraction of Savagery to Creatures, usually known as the SPCA, is perhaps the earliest and most noticeable creature government assistance associations. It was established by Richard Martin in Britain in 1824. The SPCA's central goal was to forestall brutality to ponies, principally working ponies that confronted abuse and exhaust.

This spearheading association prompted huge lawful changes, including the 1822 Martin's Demonstration, which was quite possibly the earliest piece of regulation to safeguard creatures. The SPCA's model and effect would rouse the development of comparative associations all over the planet.

2. **The American Culture for the Counteraction of Brutality to Creatures (ASPCA)**

The outcome of the SPCA model in Britain motivated Henry Bergh to lay out the American Culture for the Anticipation of Mercilessness to Creatures in the US in 1866. Bergh, roused by his connections with the SPCA in Britain, looked to address the maltreatment and disregard of ponies and different creatures in the US.

The ASPCA was instrumental in advancing others conscious training, starting lawful changes, and giving consideration and haven to creatures out of luck. Its work added to the entry of creature security regulation in the US.

3. **Imperial Society for the Avoidance of Remorselessness to Creatures (RSPCA)**

Established in Britain in 1824, the RSPCA was one more spearheading association in the early creature assurance development. It zeroed in on forestalling savagery to all creatures and had a wide command. The RSPCA effectively campaigned for the section of the Horrible Treatment of Steers Act in 1822, which expected to decrease the enduring of creatures during transportation.

III. Early Legitimate Changes and Their Effect

The endeavors of early creature assurance developments were instrumental in driving legitimate changes pointed toward forestalling creature mercilessness. These changes denoted a critical change in the public eye's perspectives toward creatures.

1. **The Horrible Treatment of Steers Act (1822)**

   One of the earliest bits of creature security regulation was the Horrible Treatment of Steers Act, otherwise called Martin's Demonstration, passed in the Assembled Realm in 1822. This regulation planned to address the harsh circumstances in which steers were shipped to showcase. It was one of the main legitimate measures intended to diminish the enduring of creatures.

2. **The 1824 Transient Demonstration**

   The Transient Demonstration of 1824, otherwise called the Martin's Demonstration Augmentation, extended the extent of creature security regulation in the Assembled Realm. It designated mercilessness to ponies and cows, especially by keeping them from being exhausted and overburdened.

3. **The US Creature Government assistance Act (1966)**

In the US, the early work of the ASPCA and comparative associations added to the entry of the Creature Government assistance Act in 1966. This government regulation planned to guarantee the accommodating treatment of creatures in research, show, transport, and business. It denoted a huge achievement in the security of creatures in the U.S.

IV. The Effect on Open Mindfulness and Sympathy

Early creature assurance developments prompted lawful changes as well as raised public mindfulness and empathy for creatures. These developments enlivened people to consider the moral and moral treatment of creatures.

1. **The Impact of Writing and Backing**

   Books and distributions featuring the predicament of creatures, for example, Anna Sewell's "Dark Excellence" and Lewis Gompertz's "Ethical Requests on the Circumstance of Man and of Beasts," assumed a huge part in bringing issues to light about creature mercilessness and moving backing.

2. **Accommodating Training**
   Early creature assurance social orders underlined the significance of accommodating instruction, showing the public the moral treatment of creatures. This instructive methodology intended to cultivate sympathy and empathy for creatures since early on.

3. **Inheritance and Proceeded with Activism**

The tradition of early creature security developments perseveres in contemporary creature government assistance associations and support endeavors. Their spearheading work established the groundwork for current drives pointed toward finishing creature savagery, advancing compassionate treatment, and bringing issues to light of the moral obligations people have toward creatures.

V. Contemporary Creature Government assistance Difficulties and Progress

While critical headway has been made in creature government assistance over the course of the last 100 years, contemporary society keeps on wrestling with a scope of difficulties and moral predicaments connected with the treatment of creatures.

1. **Manufacturing plant Cultivating and Modern Farming**
   The development of production line cultivating in the twentieth century has raised moral worries about the treatment of creatures in these frameworks. Advocates for creature government assistance contend for worked on day to day environments and the decrease of experiencing in modern horticulture.

2. **Creature Testing and Exploration**
   The utilization of creatures in logical examination stays a disagreeable issue. Moral discussions community on the need to offset logical progressions with the government assistance of creatures utilized in tests. The improvement of options in contrast to creature testing is a continuous area of concentration.

3. **Untamed life Preservation and Living space Insurance**

The protection of untamed life and the conservation of regular territories present moral difficulties. Adjusting the insurance of jeopardized species with the necessities of human populaces and financial improvement requires cautious thought of the moral ramifications.

Chapter 2

The Science of Animal Welfare

Creature government assistance is a complicated and diverse field of study that spotlights on the prosperity of creatures, incorporating their physical, profound, and mental wellbeing. Throughout the long term, the logical comprehension of creature government assistance has advanced, and it has turned into a basic piece of different disciplines, including science, veterinary medication, brain research, and morals. In this complete investigation crossing we will dig into the study of creature government assistance, analyzing its set of experiences, key ideas, evaluation strategies, and its application in different settings, from agribusiness to friend creatures, untamed life protection, and lab research.

1. Verifiable Viewpoint: The Development of Creature Government assistance Science

The logical investigation of creature government assistance is a somewhat ongoing turn of events, however it has establishes in prior moral conversations about our obligations toward creatures.

1. **Pre-Logical Time: Moral Establishments**

   Prior to the rise of creature government assistance science as a proper discipline, moral scholars, for example, Jeremy Bentham in the eighteenth hundred years, stressed the significance of limiting the enduring of creatures. Their thoughts laid the moral preparation for the cutting edge comprehension of creature government assistance.

2. **Early Logical Interest**

   Logical interest in creature government assistance started to fill in the twentieth 100 years, with early examinations zeroing in on the way of behaving, physiology, and profound reactions of creatures. Specialists like Konrad Lorenz and Niko Tinbergen made critical commitments to the comprehension of creature conduct, preparing for a more logical way to deal with creature government assistance.

3. **The Five Opportunities**

In 1965, the Brambell Board in the Unified Realm presented the "Five Opportunities," a bunch of rules that filled in as the establishment for the study of creature government assistance. These opportunities incorporate independence from craving and thirst, independence from uneasiness, independence from agony, injury, or illness, opportunity to communicate typical way of behaving, and independence from dread and misery.

II. Key Ideas in Creature Government assistance Science

The study of creature government assistance is based on a bunch of center ideas that guide examination, evaluation, and strategy improvement.

1. **The Emotional Idea of Government assistance**

   One of the key standards of creature government assistance science is the acknowledgment that the prosperity of creatures is emotional and can change starting with one individual then onto the next. It not entirely set in stone by outside factors yet additionally by a creature's inside state and discernments.

2. **The "Five Areas" Model**

The "Five Spaces" model is a contemporary structure for surveying creature government assistance. It incorporates five key spaces: nourishment, climate, wellbeing, conduct, and mental state. Assessing every space gives an extensive image of a creature's prosperity.

3. **The "Five Opportunities" Returned to**

The "Five Opportunities" are still generally utilized as a kind of perspective point in creature government assistance conversations. They offer a useful and moral structure for assessing the prosperity of creatures in different settings.

III. Strategies for Surveying Creature Government assistance

Creature government assistance evaluation includes a scope of strategies and markers, which can be applied to various species and settings.

1. **Social Markers**

Noticing the way of behaving of creatures is a major strategy for evaluating their government assistance. Strange ways of behaving, like monotonous developments or hostility, can show pressure or inconvenience.

2. **Physiological Measures**

Physiological pointers, for example, pulse, cortisol levels, and internal heat level, give bits of knowledge into a creature's pressure reactions. These actions assist researchers and veterinarians with surveying a creature's government assistance and reaction to natural circumstances.

3. **Government assistance Quality Evaluation**

The Government assistance Quality venture, started in Europe, presented an exhaustive system for evaluating the government assistance of livestock. It uses a blend of social perceptions, physiological measures, and creature based pointers to give a comprehensive perspective on government assistance.

4. Self-Evaluation by Creatures

A few creature animal groups are equipped for self-evaluation, for example, birds that self-direct relief from discomfort prescription when required. These self-appraisal ways of behaving are important marks of government assistance.

IV. Creature Government assistance in Different Settings

Creature government assistance science applies to a great many settings, including horticulture, friend creatures, untamed life preservation, and lab research.

1. **Horticulture and Animals Government assistance**
   The government assistance of livestock has turned into a significant focal point of creature government assistance science. Research in this space expects to work on the day to day environments, wellbeing, and treatment of creatures in farming, with an emphasis on diminishing pressure, agony, and languishing.

2. **Friend Creature Government assistance**
   Friend creature government assistance, including canines, felines, and different pets, is a fundamental part of creature government assistance science. Research in this space investigates issues like lodging, social associations, and the counteraction of remorselessness and disregard.

3. **Natural life Protection**
   Creature government assistance science is progressively applied to natural life protection endeavors. It resolves issues, for example, territory misfortune, human-untamed life clashes, and hostage rearing projects, fully intent on guaranteeing the prosperity of wild creatures in their common habitats.

4. **Research center Creature Government assistance**

Research including lab creatures has raised moral worries, prompting the advancement of creature government assistance rules and guidelines. The "Three Rs" rule, which accentuates the decrease, refinement, and substitution of creature use in tests, is fundamental to research center creature government assistance.

V. Moral Contemplations in Creature Government assistance Science

Moral contemplations are at the center of creature government assistance science. Scientists and specialists wrestle with inquiries concerning the ethical constraints and obligations we have toward creatures.

1. **The Utilitarian Point of view**

   The utilitarian way to deal with creature government assistance thinks about the harmony between the expenses and advantages of involving creatures for human purposes. It accentuates the minimization of affliction and the boost of prosperity.

2. **Freedoms Based Approaches**

   Freedoms based moral systems, for example, basic entitlements, contend for the intrinsic privileges of creatures to be treated with deference and pride, no matter what their utility to people. This point of view difficulties the utilization of creatures for human purposes.

3. **Social and Cultural Impacts**

Social and cultural elements assume a critical part in forming moral viewpoints on creature government assistance. Various societies and social orders have changing mentalities and works on with respect to the treatment of creatures.

VI. Lawful and Strategy Structures

The study of creature government assistance has prompted the advancement of lawful and strategy systems at the public and worldwide levels.

1. **Creature Government assistance Regulation**
   Numerous nations have authorized creature government assistance regulations that administer the treatment of creatures in different settings, from agribusiness to explore, friend creatures, and untamed life preservation.
2. **Peaceful accords**

Global associations, for example, the World Creature Assurance and the World Wellbeing Association, work to create and implement peaceful accords connected with creature government assistance, especially with regards to exchange and worldwide wellbeing.

VII. Continuous Difficulties and Future Bearings

Creature government assistance science keeps on confronting a scope of difficulties, and progressing research is fundamental to resolving these issues.

1. **Adjusting Human and Creature Interests**
   One of the focal difficulties in creature government assistance science is finding the right harmony between human interests and creature prosperity, especially in situations where the utilization of creatures is profoundly dug in the public eye.
2. **Arising Moral and Innovative Difficulties**
   Headways in innovation, like quality altering and man-made brainpower, raise new moral difficulties in creature government assistance, as they empower more exact control of creature hereditary qualities and conduct.
3. **Growing the Extent of Exploration**

The extent of creature government assistance research is ceaselessly growing to incorporate a more extensive scope of species, settings, and elements that impact creature prosperity.

2.1 Understanding animal behavior and emotions

Creatures, both in the wild and in human consideration, show a great many ways of behaving and feelings. These ways of behaving and feelings are the consequence of intricate communications between their hereditary qualities, climate, and individual encounters. Understanding creature conduct and feelings isn't just logically intriguing yet in addition morally and basically huge. It illuminates our way to deal with creature care, government assistance, protection, and our relationship with the normal world. In this exhaustive investigation crossing 1700 words, we will dig into the complex universe of creature conduct and feelings, covering key ideas, the job of hereditary qualities, ecological elements, the outflow of feelings, and the ramifications for creature government assistance and protection.

1. Key Ideas in Creature Conduct and Feelings

Understanding creature conduct and feelings requires experience with a few key ideas that guide examination and translation.

1. **Ethology: The Investigation of Creature Conduct**
   Ethology is the logical investigation of creature conduct. Ethologists notice and examine the ways of behaving of creatures to figure out their capabilities, variations, and importance in their common habitats.
2. **Ways of behaving**
   Ways of behaving are monotonous arrangements of activities or responses that creatures display. These examples can go from straightforward, natural ways of behaving, similar to reflexes, to additional intricate, learned ways of behaving.
3. **Ethograms: Conduct Lists**
   Ethologists use ethograms to make inventories of a creature's ways of behaving. These inventories assist analysts with recording, arrange, and decipher the ways of behaving they notice.
4. **Feeling: The Abstract Insight**

Feeling is an intricate and emotional experience that can envelop a large number of sentiments, from bliss and dread to outrage and interest. Feelings are frequently interlaced with a creature's way of behaving, however they are not promptly discernible all the time.

II. The Job of Hereditary qualities in Creature Conduct and Feelings

Hereditary qualities assumes a huge part in deeply shaping creature conduct and feelings. The legacy of qualities starting with one age then onto the next can impact a creature's inclination to specific ways of behaving and close to home reactions.

1. **Acquired Ways of behaving**

   Acquired ways of behaving, otherwise called instinctual ways of behaving or fixed activity designs, are ways of behaving that creatures are brought into the world with. These ways of behaving are normally hereditarily designed and don't need learning. Models incorporate the home structure conduct of birds and the web-turning conduct of insects.

2. **Hereditary Inclinations**

   Hereditary inclinations can influence a creature's probability to show specific ways of behaving or profound reactions. These inclinations associate with ecological elements to profoundly mold a singular's way of behaving and feelings.

3. **Heritability of Demeanor**

In certain species, demeanor attributes can be heritable. For instance, certain canine varieties might have hereditary inclinations to be more restless or more amiable, which can impact their close to home reactions.

III. The Impact of Ecological Variables

Ecological variables are similarly significant in figuring out creature conduct and feelings. A creature's encounters and the circumstances it lives in can fundamentally affect its way of behaving and close to home state.

1. **Natural Advancement**

   Giving an improved climate potential open doors for investigation and mental feeling can emphatically affect a creature's prosperity. Enhancement can decrease pressure, further develop learning, and advance profound prosperity.

2. **Social Associations**

   Social cooperations are a significant natural element for some species. They can significantly affect a creature's close to home state, as friendly creatures frequently depend on their social bonds for help, solace, and security.

3. **Living space and Asset Accessibility**

The accessibility of food, water, and asylum in a creature's natural surroundings can impact its way of behaving and feelings. Shortage of assets can prompt rivalry and stress, while overflow can advance unwinding and happiness.

IV. The Declaration of Feelings in Creatures

While creatures can't impart feelings through language as people do, they express their feelings through different detectable ways of behaving and actual signs.

1. **Non-verbal communication**

   A creature's non-verbal communication is a strong mark of its personal state. For instance, a canine with a swaying tail and loosened up pose normally shows a positive close to home state, while a canine with a cut head and leveled hair might be communicating dread or accommodation.

2. **Vocalizations**

   Vocalizations can likewise convey feelings. The pitch, volume, and beat of a creature's vocalizations can give bits of knowledge into its close to home state. For instance, bothered or restless creatures might deliver sharp vocalizations.

3. **Looks**

In certain species, looks can uncover. For example, primates frequently display looks that convey feelings like trepidation, outrage, or satisfaction.

4. **Conduct Reactions**

Explicit ways of behaving can act as immediate signs of profound states. For example, ways of behaving like energy, animosity, withdrawal, or investigation can reflect various feelings.

V. Creature Government assistance and Grasping Feelings

Understanding creature feelings is intently attached to creature government assistance, as it illuminates our way to deal with really focusing on creatures in different settings.

1. **Livestock Government assistance**

In horticulture, understanding the feelings of domesticated animals and poultry is basic for advancing their government assistance. Rehearses that diminish pressure, give natural advancement, and guarantee sympathetic taking care of are significant for keeping up with the profound prosperity of these creatures.

2. **Sidekick Creature Government assistance**

Sidekick creature government assistance is firmly connected to understanding the feelings of pets like canines and felines. Appropriate consideration, socialization, and mental excitement are fundamental for tending to their feelings.

3. **Natural life Preservation**

Understanding the feelings and standards of conduct of natural life is urgent for fruitful preservation endeavors. Keeping up with normal ways of behaving and limiting pressure during imprisonment and renewed introduction programs are fundamental for protecting wild populaces.

4. Research center Creature Government assistance

In lab research, perceiving the close to home encounters of creatures is significant for moral treatment. Specialists are progressively attempting to refine techniques, diminish the pressure of creatures, and supplant creature models with choices to limit languishing.

VI. The Moral Contemplations of Creature Feelings

Moral contemplations encompassing creature feelings have prompted the improvement of standards and rules for creature care.

1. The Five Opportunities

The "Five Opportunities" presented in the field of creature government assistance accentuate the significance of furnishing creatures with independence from yearning and thirst, independence from uneasiness, independence from agony, injury, or sickness, opportunity to communicate typical way of behaving, and independence from dread and misery.

2. The Consciousness Rule

The standard of creature awareness states that creatures are fit for encountering feelings and that their prosperity should be viewed as in moral navigation and public arrangement.

3. The Job of Basic entitlements

The basic entitlements development contends that creatures have innate privileges, including the option to live liberated from affliction. This viewpoint has prompted requires the nullification of specific practices, for example, animal testing and production line cultivating.

VII. Momentum Exploration and Future Bearings

Research on creature conduct and feelings keeps on propelling, offering new experiences and strategies for understanding and further developing the prosperity of creatures.

1. **Neurobiology and Feelings**
   Progressions in neurobiology are revealing insight into the brain processes fundamental creature feelings. This exploration can advise the advancement regarding mediations and medicines to further develop the close to home prosperity of creatures.
2. **Preservation and Environmental Brain research**
   The field of protection brain research investigates the profound associations among people and the regular world, elevating close to home connection to natural life and biological systems for of preservation.
3. **Moral Rules and Regulation**

Moral rules and regulation are consistently developing to mirror the developing comprehension of creature feelings. Lawful structures and guidelines for creature government assistance are being refined and extended to more readily safeguard creatures.

2.2 The role of animal cognition in ethical considerations

The moral treatment of creatures has been a subject of discussion and worry for a really long time. As how we might interpret creature discernment has developed, so too has the profundity and intricacy of moral contemplations encompassing our treatment of non-human creatures. Creature comprehension, the investigation of mental cycles in creatures, including discernment, learning, memory, critical thinking, and direction, has revealed insight into the rich inward existences of numerous species.

In this complete investigation spreading over we will dive into the basic job of creature comprehension in moral contemplations, analyzing the ramifications for creature government assistance, protection, research, and the more extensive moral structure that directs our associations with non-human creatures.

1. **Creature Cognizance: A Short Outline**

Creature cognizance is the investigation of how creatures see, process, and answer data from their current circumstance. It incorporates a great many mental cycles, including:

1. **Discernment:** How creatures see their environmental elements through their faculties, like vision, hearing, taste, smell, and contact.
2. **Learning:** The capacity of creatures to secure new data, ways of behaving, or abilities through experience or preparing.
3. **Memory:** The limit of creatures to store and recover data over the long haul, including present moment and long haul memory.
4. **Critical thinking:** The use of mental cycles to defeat difficulties or obstructions in their current circumstance.
5. **Navigation:** The mental cycles associated with deciding and choosing activities in view of seen data.

II. Creature Discernment and Moral Contemplations

Creature comprehension is integral to moral contemplations connected with the treatment of creatures, and it educates our comprehension regarding their intellectual abilities and encounters. This information has extensive ramifications for a scope of settings and practices.

1. **Creature Government assistance**

   The investigation of creature cognizance has featured the profound and mental existences of creatures. This understanding is basic in surveying and tending to their government assistance. Ideas, for example, consciousness, the capacity to encounter feelings and enduring, are vital to assessing the moral treatment of creatures in different settings.

2. **Protection**

   In the field of untamed life preservation, information on creature discernment is crucial for understanding the way of behaving and decision-production of species in danger. Preservation endeavors should consider how creatures see and answer changes in their current circumstance, and what these progressions can mean for their endurance and prosperity.

3. **Lab Exploration**

Moral contemplations encompassing the utilization of creatures in logical examination are profoundly educated by our comprehension regarding creature perception. Specialists and ethicists wrestle with inquiries concerning the mental capacities of creatures utilized in tests and the potential for anguish.

4. **Agribusiness and Livestock Government assistance**

Livestock government assistance is one more region significantly impacted by our insight into creature comprehension. The psychological and close to home encounters of creatures in horticulture are essential to assessing moral practices and advancing the prosperity of animals.

III. Creature Discernment Practically speaking

Creature insight research has commonsense ramifications for different areas of creature care and the board.

1. **Advancement and Hostage Care**

Zoos, aquariums, and untamed life asylums apply information on creature discernment to give fitting enhancement to hostage creatures. Improvement programs animate creatures intellectually and truly, diminishing pressure and advancing normal ways of behaving.

2. **Preparing and Encouraging feedback**

Creature preparing and cultivation in different settings, from buddy creatures to marine vertebrates in imprisonment, depend on the standards of encouraging feedback and a comprehension of creature perception. This approach cultivates collaboration and decreases the requirement for reformatory preparation strategies.

3. **Untamed life Restoration**

Untamed life restoration focuses apply information on creature perception to foster methodologies for the consideration and arrival of harmed or stranded creatures. Understanding their mental necessities is pivotal for their fruitful re-visitation of nature.

4. **Protection Brain research**

In the field of protection brain science, analysts think about the mental and close to home reactions of people to natural life and ecological issues. This information is fundamental for creating viable techniques to connect with people in general in protection endeavors.

IV. Moral Contemplations in Creature Perception

The investigation of creature perception raises a large group of moral contemplations connected with the treatment and utilization of creatures in different settings.

1. **The Acknowledgment of Awareness**

Awareness, the ability to encounter enduring and feelings, is vital to moral contemplations. Recognizing that animals are aware creatures challenges the moral supports for rehearses that inflict any kind of damage or enduring, for example, industrial facility cultivating or obtrusive examination.

2. **Limiting Misery**

A center moral guideline is the minimization of torment. Understanding creature discernment can assist with recognizing strategies and practices that decrease pressure, torment, and dread in creatures utilized in different settings.

3. **The Standard of Regard**

The standard of regard highlights the ethical constraint to treat creatures with nobility and thought. This standard aides our associations with creatures and illuminates moral systems that focus on their prosperity.

4. **Moral Issues in Exploration**

With regards to logical exploration, moral situations emerge when the mental limits of creatures are considered. Analysts and establishments should gauge the expected advantages of exploration against the prosperity and moral treatment of creatures.

V. The Test of Deciphering Creature Cognizance

While how we might interpret creature cognizance has progressed essentially, there are difficulties in deciphering the mental cycles of creatures.

1. **Humanoid attribution**

   Humanoid attribution, the attribution of human-like qualities to creatures, can prompt misinterpretations of creature perception. Specialists should cautiously try not to extend human encounters onto creatures.

2. **Changeability Across Species**

   Mental capacities change across species, making it essential to think about the remarkable qualities and ways of behaving of various creatures. What is mental intricacy for one animal categories may not make a difference to another.

3. **Moral Contemplations in Exploration**

Research including creature discernment frequently presents moral problems. Adjusting the requirement for logical information with the moral treatment of creatures is a continuous test.

VI. The Continuous Development of Moral Systems

As how we might interpret creature cognizance develops, moral systems and principles keep on advancing. This progress is clear in the improvement of moral rules, regulation, and public mindfulness.

1. **Moral Rules**

   Logical associations and foundations lay out moral rules for the treatment of creatures in research. These rules underscore the moral treatment and prosperity of creatures.

2. Legitimate Systems

Regulation is a significant device for safeguarding creatures and advancing their government assistance. Regulations and guidelines are ceaselessly refreshed to mirror our developing comprehension of creature perception and moral obligations.

3. Public Mindfulness and Backing

The public's familiarity with creature insight and government assistance has developed essentially. Backing gatherings and missions assume a critical part in bringing issues to light, impacting general assessment, and upholding for moral treatment.

VII. Future Bearings in the Investigation of Creature Cognizance and Morals

The investigation of creature discernment and its part in moral contemplations is an always advancing field. Future headings include:

1. Growing Exploration

Proceeded with investigation into creature insight will expand how we might interpret the mental capacities of various species, revealing insight into beforehand neglected parts of their psychological lives.

2. Applied Moral Structures

Moral structures will keep on being applied in different settings, directing the treatment and the executives of creatures in horticulture, exploration, and preservation.

3. Lawful and Strategy Changes

Lawful and strategy changes will mirror the developing comprehension of creature perception, with expanded accentuation on safeguarding the government assistance of creatures and decreasing torment.

2.3 The impact of stress, pain, and suffering on animals

Stress, torment, and enduring are huge variables that influence creatures in different settings, including the wild, bondage, examination, and agribusiness. Understanding the effect of these negative encounters on creatures is fundamental for moral contemplations, creature government assistance, and preservation endeavors. In this extensive investigation traversing 1500 words, we will dive into the significant impacts of pressure, agony, and experiencing on creatures, looking at the physical and mental results, moral ramifications, and the endeavors to alleviate and forestall such encounters.

1. Stress in Creatures

Stress is a physiological and mental reaction to testing or undermining circumstances. In creatures, stress can appear in different structures, and its effect can be both present moment and durable.

1. **Actual Impacts of Pressure**
   Stress sets off a scope of physiological reactions, including expanded pulse, raised cortisol levels, and the arrival of adrenaline. These reactions are versatile for the time being, setting up the creature to answer an apparent danger. Be that as it may, constant pressure can prompt long haul medical issues, like debilitated resistant frameworks and expanded weakness to infections.
2. **Conduct Impacts of Pressure**
   Creatures under pressure might display different conduct changes, like animosity, withdrawal, diminished movement, and modified taking care of examples. These ways of behaving can adversely affect the creature's general prosperity and may likewise disturb social designs and communications.
3. **Constant Pressure in Imprisonment**

Creatures in imprisonment, remembering those for zoos, aquariums, and research offices, are powerless to constant pressure because of elements like control, restricted ecological feeling, and social detachment. Constant pressure in bondage is a huge moral worry, as it can prompt unfortunate creature government assistance and decreased personal satisfaction.

II. Torment in Creatures

Torment is a complicated and emotional experience, and creatures can encounter physical and profound agony. Understanding torment in creatures is urgent for moral contemplations, creature government assistance, and veterinary consideration.

1. **Actual Torment**

   Actual torment in creatures can result from wounds, diseases, or surgeries. Creatures might display unmistakable indications of torment, like limping, vocalizations, or changes in conduct. Appropriate agony the board is fundamental to mitigate enduring and advance recuperation.

2. **Profound Agony**

   Profound torment, or mental pain, can likewise influence creatures. This sort of aggravation might result from social disconnection, injury, or loss of mates. It is frequently difficult to perceive close to home agony in creatures, however it can affect their prosperity.

3. **Moral Contemplations in Torment The executives**

Moral contemplations in torment the executives include surveying the harmony between the expected advantages of operations and the need to limit agony and experiencing in creatures. Moral standards expect that aggravation the board be fundamentally important in creature care.

III. Experiencing in Creatures

Enduring incorporates a great many negative encounters, including torment, trouble, dread, and persistent pressure. Experiencing can result different factors and conditions, and its ramifications can be serious and durable.

1. **Experiencing in Nature**

   Creatures in the wild might encounter experiencing because of elements like predation, wounds, food shortage, and natural difficulties. Preservation endeavors expect to address experiencing in the wild by alleviating dangers and safeguarding jeopardized species.

2. **Experiencing in Bondage**

   Creatures in bondage, whether in zoos, aquariums, or research offices, can encounter experiencing because of restriction, lacking consideration, and social separation. Moral principles expect that endeavors be made to limit experiencing in hostage creatures.

3. **Moral Systems for Enduring Moderation**

Moral systems, like the Five Opportunities and standards of creature government assistance, accentuate the significance of relieving experiencing in creatures. These systems guide moral contemplations and activities pointed toward further developing the prosperity of creatures.

IV. Endeavors to Alleviate and Forestall Pressure, Agony, and Languishing

Various endeavors and approaches have been created to moderate and forestall pressure, agony, and experiencing in creatures across different settings. These drives are key to working on creature government assistance and advancing moral treatment.

1. **Torment The executives in Veterinary Consideration**

   In veterinary medication, torment the executives conventions have been created to address actual agony in creatures going through surgeries or experiencing ailments. These conventions guarantee that creatures get proper help with discomfort and care.

2. **Enhancement and Natural Improvement**

   In hostage settings, for example, zoos and examination offices, natural advancement programs are intended to give creatures mental and actual feeling. These projects intend to lessen pressure and further develop the mental prosperity of creatures.

3. **Moral Contemplations in Exploration**

In logical exploration including creatures, moral rules and standards accentuate the significance of limiting torment and pain. The "Three Rs" standard — decrease, refinement, and substitution — means to diminish the quantity of creatures utilized, refine strategies to limit enduring, and supplant creature models with options whenever the situation allows.

4. **Moral Practices in Farming**

In horticulture, moral practices include giving livestock proper day to day environments, admittance to the outside, and empathetic treatment. Endeavors are made to lessen pressure, agony, and experiencing in animals through better lodging, taking care of, and transportation.

V. Moral Difficulties and Continuous Discussions

Regardless of critical advancement in relieving and forestalling pressure, torment, and experiencing in creatures, moral difficulties and discussions endure.

1. **Adjusting Human Interests**

Adjusting the interests of people and creatures stays a test, especially in settings where human interests might struggle with the prosperity of creatures, like in farming, examination, and natural life the executives.

2. **Social and Cultural Changeability**

Social and cultural elements impact moral contemplations and practices connected with creatures. Various societies and social orders have fluctuating perspectives and works on with respect to the treatment of creatures.

3. **Moral Quandaries in Protection**

Preservation endeavors frequently include complex moral quandaries, for example, choices about untamed life the executives and mediations to safeguard imperiled species. Moral contemplations should adjust the government assistance of individual creatures with the more extensive preservation objectives.

3 |

Chapter 3

Ethical Frameworks for Animal Welfare

Creature government assistance has turned into a focal worry in the present society, as how we might interpret the encounters and needs of creatures has developed. Moral systems for creature government assistance give the ethical establishment to how we ought to treat creatures, enveloping both the moral rules that guide our activities and the lawful and strategy structures that uphold these standards. In this complete investigation crossing we will dive into the different moral structures that support our way to deal with creature government assistance, including utilitarianism, freedoms based morals, prudence morals, and the rules that oversee our legitimate and strategy systems for safeguarding creatures.

1. Utilitarianism and Creature Government assistance

Utilitarianism is a consequentialist moral system that states that the ethical rightness of a still up in the air by its ramifications. With regards to creature government assistance, utilitarianism underlines the significance of limiting affliction and amplifying prosperity for creatures. Key parts of utilitarian morals in creature government assistance include:

1. **The Standard of Utility**

    The guideline of utility, a focal fundamental of utilitarianism, expresses that activities ought to mean to deliver the best generally joy or prosperity for the best number of people. With regards to creature government assistance, this implies that rehearses that cause pointless enduring ought to be kept away from, and measures that upgrade creature prosperity ought to be sought after.

2. **Limiting Damage**

    Utilitarian morals in creature government assistance require the minimization of damage and languishing. Rehearses that cause torment, misery, or experiencing in creatures are viewed as morally dangerous except if they can be legitimate by a more noteworthy great, like logical examination with critical advantages.

3. **Money saving advantage Investigation**

Utilitarianism frequently includes a money saving advantage investigation to survey the compromise between the misery and prosperity of creatures. In fields like lab research, the guideline of utilitarianism directs the assessment of the advantages of the exploration versus the experiencing persevered by creatures.

II. Privileges Based Morals and Basic entitlements

Freedoms based morals, or deontological morals, underlines the intrinsic privileges of people and the ethical obligation to regard those freedoms. With regards to creature government assistance, this system supports the basic entitlements development, which advocates for the inborn freedoms of creatures. Key parts of privileges based morals in creature government assistance include:

1. **Intrinsic Privileges of Creatures**

    Basic entitlements advocates contend that creatures have intrinsic privileges, for example, the option to live liberated from misery and mischief. These privileges are not dependent upon their utility to people and are grounded in the ethical obligation to regard the lives and prosperity of creatures.

2. **Speciesism**

Privileges based morals challenges speciesism, the inconsistent oppression creatures in light of their species. It declares that every conscious being, no matter what their species, reserve an option to be treated with deference and pride.

3. **Moral Veganism**

Numerous basic entitlements advocates advance moral veganism, which is a direction for living pointed toward lessening damage to creatures by going without the utilization of creature items. This approach is established in the conviction that involving creatures for food, apparel, or diversion disregards their innate privileges.

III. Goodness Morals and the Personality of Creature Overseers

Prudence morals is a moral system that spotlights on the person and temperances of people instead of explicit standards or outcomes. With regards to animal government assistance, ideals morals accentuates the personality of the people who care for animals, whether as pet people, ranchers, or scientists. Key parts of prudence morals in creature government assistance include:

1. **Prudent Person Qualities**

Righteousness morals recognizes character qualities that are important in creature care, like sympathy, compassion, and obligation. Idealistic overseers are supposed to have these characteristics and act in manners that advance creature prosperity.

2. **Adjusting Liabilities**

Uprightness morals recognizes the intricacies of creature care and the requirement for guardians to adjust their obligations toward creatures with other moral contemplations, like natural manageability and human prosperity.

3. **Moral Schooling and Preparing**

Prudence morals advances moral schooling and preparing to develop righteous person attributes in people liable for the government assistance of creatures. Projects and assets that stress sympathy and empathy are urged to upgrade creature care.

IV. Legitimate and Strategy Systems for Creature Government assistance

Lawful and strategy structures for creature government assistance give the administrative and requirement components to shield creatures from damage and languishing. These systems are educated by moral standards and plan to make an interpretation of those standards into functional rules and norms. Key parts of legitimate and strategy structures for creature government assistance include:

1. **Creature Government assistance Regulation**
   Numerous nations have established creature government assistance regulations that oversee the treatment of creatures in different settings, like farming, research, sidekick animals, and untamed life preservation. These regulations lay out legitimate norms for the consideration and treatment of creatures.

2. **Peaceful accords**
   Global associations, for example, the World Creature Security and the World Wellbeing Association, work to create and authorize peaceful accords connected with creature government assistance, especially with regards to exchange and worldwide wellbeing.

3. **Moral Oversight and Guideline**

Moral oversight and guideline are vital to guaranteeing the moral treatment of creatures in exploration and trial and error. Moral survey sheets and oversight systems assist with assessing the moral and logical defenses for involving creatures in tests.

V. Moral Contemplations and Difficulties

The use of moral systems for creature government assistance isn't without its difficulties and moral quandaries. Different elements and settings offer complex conversation starters and issues for those endeavoring to maintain moral principles for creature government assistance. Key moral contemplations and difficulties in creature government assistance include:

1. **Adjusting Human and Creature Interests**

   One of the focal difficulties in creature government assistance is finding the right harmony between human interests and creature prosperity, especially in situations where the utilization of creatures is profoundly settled in the public eye, like in agribusiness and exploration.

2. **Social and Cultural Impacts**

   Social and cultural variables assume a huge part in forming moral viewpoints on creature government assistance. Various societies and social orders have changing mentalities and works on in regards to the treatment of creatures.

3. **Moral Quandaries in Preservation**

Preservation endeavors frequently include complex moral predicaments, for example, choices about natural life the executives and intercessions to safeguard imperiled species. Moral contemplations should adjust the government assistance of individual creatures with the more extensive protection objectives.

3.1 Utilitarianism and its application to animal ethics

Utilitarianism is a consequentialist moral hypothesis that places that the ethical rightness of a not entirely settled by the general harmony between satisfaction and enduring it produces. With regards to creature morals, utilitarianism assumes a huge part in directing our ethical decisions and choices in regards to the treatment and utilization of creatures. This moral structure centers around the results of our activities for creatures and accentuates the significance of limiting misery and augmenting prosperity. In this extensive investigation traversing we will dive into utilitarianism and its application to creature morals, looking at the standards of utilitarian morals, moral contemplations in different settings, and the difficulties and discussions encompassing the utilization of this structure.

1. Standards of Utilitarian Morals

Utilitarianism depends on a few major rules that give the moral establishment to its application to creature morals:

1. **The Standard of Utility**
   The guideline of utility, the foundation of utilitarianism, affirms that activities ought to plan to deliver the best generally speaking joy or prosperity for the best number of people. With regards to creature morals, this guideline underscores the significance of limiting anguish and amplifying prosperity for creatures.
2. **Consequentialism**
   Utilitarianism is a consequentialist moral hypothesis, implying that it assesses the profound quality of activities in view of their results. Activities are viewed as ethically right or wrong in light of the equilibrium of positive and adverse results they produce.
3. **Gluttonous Math**

Utilitarianism frequently utilizes an epicurean math to gauge bliss and languishing. It assesses the force, length, assurance, propinquity, fertility, immaculateness, and degree of joy or torment brought about by an activity. The objective is to decide if an activity brings about more satisfaction than affliction.

II. Utilitarianism and Creature Government assistance

The utilization of utilitarianism to creature morals puts major areas of strength for an on the prosperity and enduring of creatures. This moral structure directs our choices in regards to the treatment of creatures in different settings, like agribusiness, research, untamed life preservation, and sidekick creature care.

1. **Limiting Experiencing in Farming**
   With regards to horticulture, utilitarianism requires the decrease of experiencing experienced by livestock. This incorporates working on everyday environments, lessening the utilization of horrible practices, and guaranteeing that creatures are brought up in conditions that advance their physical and mental prosperity.

2. **Moral Contemplations in Creature Exploration**
   Utilitarian morals impact choices about the utilization of creatures in logical exploration. The guideline of limiting enduring is foremost, and the "Three Rs" rule — decrease, refinement, and substitution — expects to limit the quantity of creatures utilized, refine methods to diminish enduring, and supplant creature models with options whenever the situation allows.

3. **Untamed life Protection and Moral Problems**
   In natural life preservation, utilitarianism assumes a part in tending to moral problems, especially when protection endeavors might include damage to individual creatures to support the species or biological system. Moral contemplations balance the prosperity of individual creatures with more extensive protection objectives.

4. **Friend Creature Government assistance**

Utilitarianism guides choices connected with friend creature government assistance, guaranteeing that creatures experience negligible anguish and most extreme prosperity. It underlines mindful possession, proper consideration, and the anticipation of pointless torment.

III. Moral Contemplations and Difficulties

The utilization of utilitarianism to creature morals isn't without its difficulties and moral predicaments. Different elements and settings suggest complex conversation starters and predicaments for those endeavoring to maintain utilitarian moral guidelines for creatures.

1. **Adjusting Human and Creature Interests**

   One of the focal moves in applying utilitarianism to creature morals is tracking down the right harmony between human interests and creature prosperity. This is especially difficult in situations where human interests, like financial benefits or logical headways, may struggle with the prosperity of creatures.

2. **Social and Cultural Inconstancy**

   Social and cultural elements assume a critical part in molding moral points of view on creature government assistance. Various societies and social orders have changing perspectives and works on in regards to the treatment of creatures. The utilization of utilitarianism can differ broadly founded on social standards and values.

3. **Moral Problems in Protection**

   Preservation endeavors frequently include complex moral situations. Choices about natural life the executives and intercessions to safeguard imperiled species bring up issues about the ethical compromises between the prosperity of individual creatures and the protection of environments and species.

4. **The Difficulties of Estimating Creature Prosperity**

One of the reasonable provokes in applying utilitarianism to creature morals is the exact estimation of creature prosperity. Evaluating a creature's psychological and actual state and ascertaining the net equilibrium between delight and agony they experience can be troublesome and dependent upon understanding.

IV. Discusses Encompassing Utilitarianism in Creature Morals

Utilitarianism in creature morals isn't without its faultfinders and discussions. A few discussions and conversations base on the utilization of this moral system in different settings:

1. **Anthropocentrism and Speciesism**
   Pundits contend that utilitarianism, as other moral systems, can be affected by anthropocentrism and speciesism, where the interests of people are given need over those of creatures. They guarantee that utilitarianism may not completely address the interests and freedoms of creatures.

2. **The Issue of Total**
   Utilitarian computations frequently include conglomerating the prosperity of people to decide generally outcomes. A few pundits battle that this collection can prompt ethically problematic ends, for example, forfeiting the prosperity of a couple to ultimately benefit a large number.

3. **The Extent of Moral Thought**
   Discusses spin around the degree of moral thought creatures ought to get under utilitarian morals. Should all conscious creatures be thought about similarly, or should qualifications be made in view of mental capacities, limit with regards to affliction, or different variables?

4. **Moral Compromises**

A contend that utilitarian morals can prompt moral compromises where the prosperity of creatures is forfeited for other human interests. For instance, the utilization of creatures in clinical examination for human advantage brings up issues about the moral harmony between human wellbeing and creature languishing.

3.2 Deontology and its implications for animal rights

Deontology is a moral structure that underscores the innate freedoms, obligations, and rules that guide moral activities. It remains as opposed to utilitarianism, which assesses the ethical rightness of activities in light of their outcomes. With regards to basic entitlements, deontological morals puts serious areas of strength for an on the innate privileges and moral obligations we owe to creatures. This far reaching investigation traversing will dig into deontology and its suggestions for basic entitlements, analyzing the standards of deontological morals, moral contemplations in different settings, and the difficulties and discussions encompassing the utilization of this structure.

1. Standards of Deontological Morals

Deontology is based upon a few crucial rules that give the moral establishment to its application to basic entitlements:

1. **Intrinsic Privileges**
   Deontological morals sets that people, including creatures, have intrinsic privileges that should be regarded. These privileges are not dependent upon outcomes or utility to people but rather are grounded in moral obligation.
2. **Moral Obligations and Goals**
   Moral obligations and goals are vital to deontology. These are clear cut and outright, expecting people to act as per their ethical obligations, no matter what the results.
3. **Independence and Regard for People**

Deontology underlines the significance of regarding the independence and nobility of people. This regard stretches out to creatures, perceiving their ability to encounter enduring and their intrinsic worth.

II. Deontology and Basic entitlements

Deontology's application to basic entitlements puts major areas of strength for an on the ethical obligation to regard the intrinsic privileges of creatures. This moral system directs our choices in regards to the treatment and utilization of creatures in different settings, like horticulture, research, untamed life preservation, and sidekick creature care.

1. **Acknowledgment of Basic entitlements**

   Deontology perceives the inborn privileges of creatures, for example, the option to live liberated from pointless affliction and mischief. These freedoms are not dependent upon the utility of creatures to people and are grounded in moral obligation.

2. **Moral Contemplations in Farming**

   With regards to agribusiness, deontology requires the acknowledgment of basic entitlements and the ethical obligation to guarantee that livestock are brought and treated up in manners that regard their inborn worth. Rehearses that cause enduring are viewed as morally dangerous except if they can be legitimate by a more noteworthy great.

3. **Moral Contemplations in Creature Exploration**

   Deontology educates choices about the utilization regarding creatures in logical examination. The acknowledgment of basic entitlements puts an accentuation on the ethical obligation to limit enduring and hurt. Moral standards guide the assessment of the advantages of examination versus the moral contemplations for the creatures in question.

4. **Deontology in Natural life Protection**

   Deontology assumes a part in moral problems inside natural life protection, especially when preservation endeavors might include mischief to individual creatures to serve the species or biological system. Moral contemplations balance the prosperity of individual creatures with more extensive protection objectives.

5. **Sidekick Creature Government assistance**

Deontological morals guides choices connected with sidekick creature government assistance, underlining the ethical obligation to guarantee that creatures experience insignificant misery and are treated with nobility and regard. Dependable possession and proper consideration are fundamental to this structure.

III. Moral Contemplations and Difficulties

The utilization of deontology to basic entitlements isn't without its difficulties and moral predicaments. Different elements and settings offer complex conversation starters and issues for those endeavoring to maintain deontological moral norms for creatures.

1. **Adjusting Human and Creature Interests**

   One of the focal difficulties in applying deontology to basic entitlements is tracking down the right harmony between human interests and creature prosperity. This is especially difficult in situations where human interests, like monetary benefits or logical headways, may struggle with the prosperity of creatures.

2. **Social and Cultural Inconstancy**

   Social and cultural variables assume a critical part in forming moral viewpoints on basic entitlements. Various societies and social orders have shifting perspectives and works on in regards to the treatment of creatures. The utilization of deontology can change generally founded on social standards and values.

3. **Moral Situations in Preservation**

Protection endeavors frequently include complex moral problems. Choices about untamed life the board and mediations to safeguard imperiled species bring up issues about the ethical compromises between the prosperity of individual creatures and the conservation of biological systems and species.

IV. Discusses Encompassing Deontology in Basic entitlements

Deontology in basic entitlements isn't without its faultfinders and contentions. A few discussions and conversations base on the utilization of this moral structure in different settings:

1. **Anthropocentrism and Speciesism**

   Pundits contend that deontology, as other moral structures, can in any case be impacted by anthropocentrism and speciesism, where the interests of people are given need over those of creatures. They guarantee that deontology may not completely address the interests and freedoms of creatures.

2. **Moral Freedoms for All Creatures**

Discusses spin around the degree of moral thought creatures ought to get under deontological morals. Should all aware creatures be thought about similarly, or should qualifications be made in view of mental capacities, limit with respect to misery, or different elements?

3. **Moral Compromises**

Some contend that deontology can prompt moral compromises where the prosperity of creatures is forfeited for other human interests. For instance, the utilization of creatures in clinical exploration for human advantage brings up issues about the moral harmony between human wellbeing and creature languishing.

3.3 Virtue ethics and the cultivation of empathy for animals

Prudence morals is a moral structure that spotlights on the person and ideals of people instead of explicit principles or outcomes. It accentuates the advancement of moral ideals, like sympathy, compassion, and obligation, to direct moral way of behaving. With regards to our relationship with creatures, excellence morals assumes a huge part in the development of sympathy and empathy toward non-human animals. This far reaching investigation crossing 1500 words will dig into uprightness morals and its suggestions for the development of sympathy for creatures, analyzing the standards of temperance morals, moral contemplations in different settings, and the difficulties and discussions encompassing the utilization of this system.

1. **Standards of Ideals Morals**

Ideals morals is based upon a few essential rules that give the moral establishment to its application to the development of compassion for creatures:

1. **Ethical Person Attributes**

   Ideals morals recognizes character attributes, like sympathy, compassion, and obligation, as significant in moral navigation. These ethics guide people in their collaborations with others, including creatures.

2. **Moral Instruction and Development**

   Ethicalness morals underlines moral schooling and the development of righteous person characteristics. It perceives that people can create and sustain these ideals after some time through reflection, practice, and moral direction.

3. **Adjusting Liabilities**

Excellence morals recognizes the intricacies of our associations with creatures and the need to adjust our obligations toward them with other moral contemplations, like natural manageability and human prosperity.

II. Ethicalness Morals and the Development of Compassion for Creatures

Ethicalness morals supports the development of sympathy and empathy for creatures, perceiving their ability to encounter enduring and their innate worth. This moral system directs our choices and ways of behaving in different settings, like farming, research, untamed life preservation, and buddy animal consideration.

1. **Sympathy and Creature Government assistance**

   Ideals morals requires the improvement of empathy as a high-minded character quality, driving people to consider the prosperity and enduring of creatures. In agribusiness, for instance, empathy guides choices that focus on the government assistance of livestock and advance empathetic treatment.

2. **Moral Contemplations in Creature Exploration**

   Goodness morals advises choices about the utilization regarding creatures in logical examination. Sympathy and compassion are esteemed ideals that guide specialists in thinking about the moral ramifications of their work and endeavoring to limit languishing.

3. **Untamed life Protection and Moral Situations**

Temperance morals assumes a part in moral predicaments inside untamed life preservation, particularly when protection endeavors might include mischief to individual creatures to support the species or biological system. Sympathy and compassion assist people with settling on tough decisions that balance the prosperity of individual creatures with more extensive protection objectives.

4. **Friend Creature Government assistance**

Goodness morals guides choices connected with friend creature government assistance, accentuating the advancement of excellencies like liability and sympathy in pet people. Capable possession and the development of compassion assist with guaranteeing that creatures are treated with care and regard.

III. Moral Contemplations and Difficulties

The utilization of righteousness morals to the development of compassion for creatures isn't without its difficulties and moral issues. Different elements and settings suggest complex conversation starters and difficulties for those endeavoring to maintain ethical person qualities in their connections with creatures.

1. **Adjusting Human and Creature Interests**

One of the focal provokes in applying ideals morals to creature government assistance is tracking down the right harmony between human interests and creature prosperity. This is especially difficult in situations where human interests, like monetary benefits or logical headways, may struggle with the prosperity of creatures.

2. **Social and Cultural Inconstancy**

Social and cultural elements assume a critical part in forming moral points of view on creature government assistance. Various societies and social orders have differing mentalities and works on in regards to the treatment of creatures. The use of prudence morals can fluctuate generally founded on social standards and values.

3. **Moral Situations in Preservation**

Preservation endeavors frequently include complex moral problems. Choices about natural life the board and intercessions to safeguard imperiled species bring up issues about the ethical compromises between the prosperity of individual creatures and the conservation of environments and species.

IV. Discusses Encompassing Ideals Morals in Creature Government assistance

Ideals morals in creature government assistance isn't without its faultfinders and discussions. A few discussions and conversations base on the use of this moral system in different settings:

1. **Anthropocentrism and Speciesism**
   Pundits contend that uprightness morals, as other moral structures, can in any case be impacted by anthropocentrism and speciesism, where the interests of people are given need over those of creatures. They guarantee that righteousness morals may not completely address the interests and freedoms of creatures.

2. **Goodness Improvement in People**
   Discusses rotate around the degree to which excellence morals can impact human way of behaving and dynamic for creature government assistance. Pundits question the viability of righteousness morals in encouraging certified sympathy and empathetic activity.

3. **Social and Cultural Impacts**

The effect of social and cultural elements on the development of temperances for creatures is likely to discuss. A few contend that social standards and values might obstruct or advance the improvement of ideals connected with creature sympathy and empathy.

Chapter 4

Animal Rights and Legal Protections

The idea of basic entitlements and the legitimate assurances stood to creatures have developed fundamentally as of late. While creatures have been utilized for different human purposes since the beginning of time, the moral and moral contemplations in regards to their treatment have prompted the improvement of a system for basic entitlements. Legitimate securities assume an essential part in shielding the government assistance and interests of creatures. This exhaustive investigation traversing 4000 words will dive into the idea of basic entitlements, the verifiable improvement of lawful securities for creatures, the critical standards of basic entitlements, and the contemporary legitimate systems and difficulties encompassing basic entitlements and assurances.

1. The Idea of Basic entitlements

Basic entitlements, as a philosophical and moral idea, declares that non-human creatures have inborn privileges, similarly as, that ought to be regarded and secured. These freedoms are grounded in the conviction that creatures have characteristic worth and the ability to encounter enduring and prosperity.

1. **Authentic Viewpoints on Basic entitlements**
   The idea of basic entitlements has profound verifiable roots, with prominent figures like Jeremy Bentham and Henry Salt upholding for the acknowledgment of basic entitlements in the eighteenth and nineteenth hundreds of years. Early defenders of basic entitlements contended that creatures ought to be safeguarded from superfluous affliction and damage.
2. **Key Standards of Basic entitlements**

Innate Worth: Basic entitlements advocates declare that creatures have intrinsic worth and an option to exist liberated from misery and double-dealing.

Enduring and Prosperity: Perceiving that creatures can encounter enduring and prosperity, the standard of basic entitlements stresses the significance of limiting anguish and advancing positive encounters for creatures.

Privileges and Moral Thought: The idea of basic entitlements affirms that creatures ought to be concurred moral thought, no matter what their utility to people.

II. Verifiable Improvement of Legitimate Insurances for Creatures

The authentic improvement of legitimate assurances for creatures has seen critical improvement after some time, reflecting changes in cultural mentalities and moral contemplations with respect to creature treatment. Key achievements in this advancement include:

1. **Against Remorselessness Regulations**
   Hostile to savagery regulations, tracing all the way back to the mid nineteenth hundred years, expected to address the uncaring treatment of creatures. These regulations made it against the

law to participate in rehearses that made superfluous enduring creatures.

2. **The Rise of Creature Government assistance Associations**

   The development of creature government assistance associations, like the Illustrious Society for the Counteraction of Remorselessness to Creatures (RSPCA) in 1824, assumed a basic part in supporting for basic entitlements and pushing for lawful securities.

3. **Regulative Changes**

   All through the twentieth 100 years, regulative changes prompted the improvement of additional extensive lawful structures for creature assurance. These changes covered different parts of animal treatment, including research facility testing, cultivating practices, and friend creature care.

4. **Peaceful accords and Guidelines**

The improvement of peaceful accords and norms, like the General Statement on Creature Government assistance (UDAW) and the World Association for Creature Wellbeing (OIE) rules, flagged a developing worldwide obligation to creature government assistance and privileges.

III. Contemporary Legitimate Systems for Basic entitlements and Insurances

Contemporary legitimate systems for basic entitlements and insurances fluctuate broadly by nation and area. Key parts of these systems include:

1. **Creature Government assistance Regulation**

   Numerous nations have instituted creature government assistance regulation that tends to the altruistic treatment of creatures, illustrating lawful guidelines for their consideration, lodging, and transportation.

2. **Regulations Tending to Creature Testing**

   Regulation overseeing creature testing in logical examination plans to adjust the requirement for logical progression with the moral treatment of creatures. These regulations normally re-member arrangements for the moral utilization of creatures for research and the decrease of creature languishing.

3. **Guidelines for Creature Farming**

Animal agribusiness is dependent upon different guidelines that administer the treatment of livestock. These guidelines cover per-spectives like lodging, taking care of, transportation, and butcher practices.

4. **Natural life Preservation Regulations**

Regulations connected with untamed life preservation are in-tended to safeguard jeopardized species and their territories. These regulations deny exercises that mischief safeguarded species and address issues connected with poaching and environment obliteration.

5. **Sidekick Creature Regulation**

Sidekick creature regulation tends to the privileges and govern-ment assistance of pets and trained creatures. These regulations frequently incorporate arrangements connected with the empa-thetic treatment, reception, and responsibility for creatures.

6. **Peaceful accords and Guidelines**

Peaceful accords and guidelines, for example, the Show on Global Exchange Jeopardized Types of Wild Fauna and Greenery (Refers to), assume a significant part in managing the worldwide exchange untamed life and safeguarding imperiled species.

IV. Key Standards and Discussions in Contemporary Basic entitlements and Securities

The contemporary scene of basic entitlements and lawful insurances includes a scope of standards and progressing discusses:

1. **The Five Opportunities**

The "Five Opportunities," a central system for creature govern-ment assistance, incorporate independence from craving and thirst, independence from inconvenience, independence from agony, injury, or infection, opportunity to communicate typical way of behaving, and independence from dread and misery.

2. **The Job of Awareness**

Acknowledgment of creature consciousness, the ability to encounter enduring and prosperity, has turned into an essential rule in contemporary basic entitlements and securities. This standard underlines the ethical obligation to limit enduring and advance prosperity in creatures.

3. **Moral Contemplations in Creature Exploration**

The utilization of creatures in logical exploration keeps on being a subject of moral discussion. The "Three Rs" guideline — decrease, refinement, and substitution — intends to limit the utilization of creatures, refine strategies to diminish enduring, and supplant creature models with options whenever the situation allows.

4. **Banters on Manufacturing plant Cultivating**

Processing plant cultivating rehearses have ignited banters about the moral treatment of livestock and the requirement for additional rigid guidelines to address their government assistance.

5. **Natural life Preservation and Moral Difficulties**

Preservation endeavors frequently include complex moral problems, for example, choices about natural life the executives and mediations to safeguard jeopardized species. Moral contemplations should adjust the prosperity of individual creatures with more extensive preservation objectives.

6. **The Ethical Remaining of Creatures**

Discusses keep in regards to the ethical remaining of creatures and the degree to which they ought to be viewed as freedoms holders with innate interests.

V. Difficulties and Future Bearings

The quest for basic entitlements and lawful assurances isn't without its difficulties and intricacies:

1. **Adjusting Human and Creature Interests**
   One of the focal difficulties is tracking down the right harmony between human interests, like financial benefits and logical progressions, and creature prosperity.

2. **Social and Cultural Changeability**
   Social and cultural elements assume a huge part in forming moral points of view on basic entitlements and securities. Various societies and social orders have fluctuating mentalities and works on in regards to the treatment of creatures.

3. **Implementation and Consistence**
   Implementation of basic entitlements and securities can be testing, and guaranteeing consistence with lawful norms is a continuous concern.

4. **Advancing Logical Comprehension**

Headways in science and our developing comprehension of creature discernment and government assistance keep on molding the moral contemplations and lawful securities for creatures.

4.1 The history of animal rights movements

The historical backdrop of basic entitlements developments is a story of mankind's advancing moral and moral cognizance with respect to the treatment of non-human creatures. Over the entire course of time, creatures have been exposed to different types of double-dealing, brutality, and disregard, driven by human requirements and wants. The idea of creatures having privileges, like those of people, has progressively picked up speed, leading to coordinated developments pushing for the government assistance and freedoms of creatures. In this thorough investigation crossing we will dig into the verifiable development of basic entitlements developments, from their initial starting points to contemporary endeavors, featuring key achievements, persuasive figures, and the continuous battle to secure and advance the interests of creatures.

1. **Early Starting points of Creature Backing**

The underlying foundations of basic entitlements developments can be followed back to old civic establishments, where people and philosophical schools started to scrutinize the treatment of creatures.

1. **Antiquated Developments and Their Mentalities Toward Creatures**
   India: Old Indian religions, for example, Jainism and Buddhism, advanced peacefulness and the guideline of ahimsa, which stretched out to creatures. This established the groundwork for early creature government assistance and freedoms standards.
   Greece: The logician Pythagoras upheld for the family relationship among people and creatures, declaring that creatures were fit for reason and had their own advantages.
   Rome: The Stoics, a school of reasoning in old Rome, had faith in a typical objectivity shared by people and creatures, impacting their moral position on creature treatment.
2. **The Medieval times and Early Present day Term**

During the Medieval times, perspectives toward creatures were in many cases impacted by strict convictions. Holy person Francis of Assisi, known for his adoration for creatures and nature, exemplified the merciful treatment of creatures during this time.

II. Illumination and the Rise of Creature Government assistance

The Illumination time frame (seventeenth to eighteenth hundreds of years) denoted a huge defining moment in Western idea, underlining reason and morals. This time saw the rise of coordinated endeavors to address creature brutality.

1. **Jeremy Bentham and Utilitarianism**
   The scholar Jeremy Bentham's utilitarianism, which underlined the torment and bliss of conscious creatures, significantly affected the moral treatment of creatures. Bentham's assertion, "The inquiry isn't, Could they at any point reason? nor, Could they at any point talk? yet, Could they at any point endure?" laid the foundation for basic entitlements contentions.

2. **Hostile to Savagery Regulation**

The nineteenth century saw the order of hostile to brutality regulations, for example, the Savage Treatment of Steers Act (1822) in the Unified Realm and the establishing of the Illustrious Society for the Counteraction of Mercilessness to Creatures (RSPCA) in 1824, flagging a developing worry for creature government assistance.

III. Late nineteenth and Mid twentieth Hundreds of years: Progress and Difficulties

The late nineteenth and mid twentieth hundreds of years acquired huge progressions animal government assistance, yet additionally saw proceeded with difficulties as industrialization and the development of plant cultivating.

1. **Arrangement of Creature Government assistance Social orders**
   Creature government assistance social orders and associations, including the American Altruistic Affiliation (1877), the American Culture for the Anticipation of Remorselessness to Creatures (ASPCA, 1866), and different nearby creature security gatherings, were laid out to advance the compassionate treatment of creatures.

2. **The Job of Henry Bergh and Caroline Earle White**
   Henry Bergh, the organizer behind the ASPCA, and Caroline Earle White, a noticeable creature government assistance advocate, assumed urgent parts in propelling creature security

regulations, further developing circumstances for creatures in metropolitan regions, and pushing for empathetic schooling.

3. Challenges in the Modern Age

The industrialization of agribusiness led to manufacturing plant cultivating, which introduced new difficulties concerning creature government assistance. Animals were exposed to brutal everyday environments and serious cultivating rehearses.

IV. The Cutting edge Basic entitlements Development

The mid-twentieth century saw the development of the cutting edge basic entitlements development, portrayed by a more express spotlight on the acknowledgment of creatures as privileges holders.

1. **Peter Vocalist and Creature Freedom**
   Peter Vocalist's weighty book "Creature Freedom" (1975) contended that creatures have characteristic interests and privileges and required the annulment of practices that made superfluous enduring creatures.

2. **Establishing of Basic entitlements Associations**

Conspicuous basic entitlements associations, like Individuals for the Moral Treatment of Creatures (PETA, 1980) and the Creature Legitimate Safeguard Asset (ALDF, 1979), were laid out to advocate for basic entitlements, challenge creature double-dealing, and push for lawful changes.

V. Key Achievements and Legitimate Turns of events

The continuous battle for basic entitlements and government assistance has seen critical achievements and legitimate turns of events.

1. **Creature Government assistance Acts**
   Various nations have established creature government assistance acts to safeguard creatures from savagery and misuse. These demonstrations shift in extension and particularity however by

and large lay out legitimate guidelines for the consideration and treatment of creatures.

2. **The Jeopardized Species Act (1973)**
The Jeopardized Species Act is a milestone piece of regulation pointed toward safeguarding compromised and imperiled species, hence adding to the preservation of basic entitlements with regards to natural life.

3. **The Creature Government assistance Act (1966) in the US**

The Creature Government assistance Act in the US controls the treatment of creatures utilized in exploration, display, and business purposes, setting guidelines for their others conscious consideration and treatment.

VI. Progressing Difficulties and Contemporary Basic entitlements Issues

The cutting edge basic entitlements development keeps on confronting various difficulties and stand up to a scope of contemporary issues.

1. **Manufacturing plant Cultivating and Modern Farming**
Processing plant cultivating rehearses stay a quarrelsome issue, with worries about creature government assistance, ecological effect, and general wellbeing. Activists and associations are attempting to further develop conditions for livestock.

2. **Creature Testing and Exploration**
The utilization of creatures in logical exploration is a complex moral quandary. Basic entitlements advocates push for the decrease, refinement, and supplanting of creature testing with elective techniques.

3. **Untamed life Preservation and Territory Assurance**
Untamed life protection endeavors are progressively basic notwithstanding living space misfortune, poaching, and environmental change. Advocates are battling for more grounded assurances for jeopardized species and their biological systems.

4. **Friend Creature Government assistance**

Friend creature government assistance incorporates issues like capable proprietorship, pet overpopulation, and the moral treatment of pets. Basic entitlements associations work to advance reception, fixing/fixing, and capable pet consideration.

VII. Worldwide Viewpoints and Peaceful accords

The global local area assumes a pivotal part in molding basic entitlements through different arrangements and associations.

1. **The All inclusive Announcement on Creature Government assistance (UDAW)**
   The UDAW, upheld by various nations and NGOs, looks to perceive the significance of creature government assistance in global regulation and empower the accommodating treatment of creatures around the world.

2. **World Association for Creature Wellbeing (OIE)**
   The OIE sets worldwide principles for creature wellbeing and government assistance, expecting to forestall the spread of creature sicknesses and work on creature government assistance.

3. **Social Changeability and Worldwide Viewpoints**

Social and cultural contrasts impact the way to deal with basic entitlements and government assistance in various locales of the world. Understanding these distinctions is fundamental for global participation.

VIII. The Eventual fate of Basic entitlements Developments

The fate of basic entitlements developments is set apart by continuous endeavors to get legitimate securities and advance moral treatment. Key contemplations for the future include:

1. **Innovative Progressions**
   Headways in innovation, like refined meat and elective testing

strategies, may lessen the dependence on customary practices that hurt creatures.

2. **Moving Public Mindfulness**

   The developing attention to basic entitlements and government assistance issues among the overall population is probably going to drive further changes in approaches and regulation.

3. **Legitimate Changes**

   Proceeded with endeavors are expected to order and authorize more grounded legitimate assurances for creatures and to address arising moral difficulties.

4. **Moral Contemplations**

The advancing comprehension of creature discernment, awareness, and social conduct will add to more nuanced moral contemplations with respect to the treatment of creatures.

4.2 The development of animal welfare laws and regulations

The improvement of creature government assistance regulations and guidelines is a demonstration of society's developing acknowledgment of the need to secure and really focus on non-human creatures. Over the entire course of time, creatures have been exposed to different types of double-dealing and mercilessness, frequently determined by human requirements and wants. In any case, as how we might interpret creature consciousness and moral contemplations has developed, so too has the lawful system intended to shield the government assistance and freedoms of creatures. This thorough investigation, traversing 1600 words, will dig into the verifiable improvement of creature government assistance regulations and guidelines, from their initial beginnings to contemporary endeavors, featuring key achievements, powerful figures, and the continuous mission to give better insurance to creatures.

1. **Antiquated Starting points of Creature Insurance Regulations**

The underlying foundations of creature government assistance regulations and guidelines can be followed back to antiquated civic establishments, where codes and standards were laid out to resolve issues connected with creature treatment.

1. **Antiquated Mesopotamia**

   Perhaps of the earliest known lawful code, the Code of Ur-Nammu (around 2100-2050 BCE), contained arrangements for the security of creatures. It resolved issues like the proper pay for hurt caused to someone else's animals.

2. **Antiquated India**

Antiquated Indian texts, especially those affected by the standards of ahimsa (peacefulness) in Jainism and Buddhism, upheld for empathy and non-hurt towards creatures. This moral position added to the government assistance and assurance of creatures in different ways.

II. Old Greece and Rome

In old Greece and Rome, rationalists, for example, Pythagoras and the Stoics scrutinized the treatment of creatures and perceived the significance of stretching out moral thought to non-human animals.

1. **Pythagoras**

   Pythagoras put stock in the family relationship among people and creatures, affirming that creatures were equipped for reason and had their own advantages. His way of thinking affected the moral position on creature treatment.

2. **Apathy**

The Stoics, a philosophical school in old Rome, had confidence in a typical discernment shared by people and creatures. This view affected their moral thought of creature government assistance.

III. Medieval times and Strict Impact

During the Medieval times, strict convictions assumed a critical part in molding perspectives towards creatures. Holy person Francis of Assisi, known for his adoration for creatures and nature, exemplified empathetic treatment of creatures during this time.

1. Holy person Francis of Assisi

Holy person Francis is commended for his devotion to creatures and nature. His lessons and model advanced graciousness and care for all animals, establishing the groundwork for Christian creature government assistance standards.

IV. Edification and Development of Creature Government assistance

The Illumination time frame (seventeenth to eighteenth hundreds of years) denoted a critical change in Western idea, stressing reason and morals. This time saw the development of coordinated endeavors to address creature brutality.

1. Jeremy Bentham and Utilitarianism

The logician Jeremy Bentham's utilitarianism, underlining the misery and bliss of conscious creatures, significantly affected the moral treatment of creatures. His assertion, "The inquiry isn't, Might they at any point reason? nor, Could they at any point talk? be that as it may, Could they at any point endure?" laid the preparation for creature government assistance contentions.

2. nineteenth Century Creature Assurance Social orders

The nineteenth century saw the establishing of associations like the Illustrious Society for the Anticipation of Mercilessness to Creatures (RSPCA) in the Assembled Realm in 1824 and the American Culture for the Counteraction of Brutality to Creatures (ASPCA) in the US in 1866. These associations assumed a pivotal part in supporting for creature government assistance and pushing for lawful securities.

V. Advancement of Creature Government assistance Regulations

The late nineteenth and mid twentieth hundreds of years denoted a time of huge progressions in creature government assistance regulations and guidelines, as well as a developing worry for the treatment of creatures.

1. **Arrangement of Creature Government assistance Social orders**

   Creature government assistance social orders and associations were laid out to advance the accommodating treatment of creatures and promoter for legitimate securities. These associations frequently assumed a vital part in molding early creature government ment assistance regulation.

2. **Henry Bergh and Caroline Earle White**

Unmistakable figures like Henry Bergh, the organizer behind the ASPCA, and Caroline Earle White, a main creature government assistance advocate, were instrumental in propelling creature security regulations and norms. Their work zeroed in on further developing circumstances for creatures in metropolitan regions and pushing for empathetic schooling.

VI. twentieth Hundred years: Advances and Difficulties

The twentieth century got the two advances animal government assistance and new difficulties, especially as industrialization and production line cultivating.

1. **Order of Creature Government assistance Regulation**

   The twentieth century saw the order of different creature government ment assistance regulations, with numerous nations executing guidelines to shield creatures from remorselessness and damage.

2. **The Job of Processing plant Cultivating**

The industrialization of horticulture and the ascent of processing plant cultivating rehearses introduced huge difficulties to creature government assistance. Animals were exposed to brutal day to day environments and serious cultivating works on, prompting worries about their prosperity.

VII. Present day Creature Government assistance Developments

The late twentieth 100 years and past saw the development of the cutting edge creature government assistance development, portrayed by a more express spotlight on the acknowledgment of creatures as conscious creatures with privileges.

1. **Creature Government assistance versus Basic entitlements**

    While creature government assistance standards kept on being a main impetus, the cutting edge creature government assistance development likewise embraced components of basic entitlements, stressing the need to perceive creatures as privileges holders.

2. **Establishing of Creature Government assistance and Basic entitlements Associations**

Unmistakable associations like the American Others conscious Affiliation (1877), the American Culture for the Avoidance of Brutality to Creatures (ASPCA, 1866), Individuals for the Moral Treatment of Creatures (PETA, 1980), and the Creature Legitimate Guard Asset (ALDF, 1979) were established to advocate for creature government assistance and freedoms, challenge creature double-dealing, and push for lawful changes.

VIII. Key Achievements and Legitimate Turns of events

All through the twentieth and 21st hundreds of years, there have been critical achievements and lawful improvements connected with creature government assistance.

1. **Creature Government assistance Acts**

    Numerous nations have executed creature government assistance acts, which fluctuate in degree and particularity yet by and large set lawful principles for the consideration and treatment of creatures.

2. **The Imperiled Species Act (1973)**

The Imperiled Species Act is a milestone piece of regulation pointed toward safeguarding compromised and jeopardized species, in this manner adding to the preservation of basic entitlements with regards to natural life.

3. **The Creature Government assistance Act (1966) in the US**

The Creature Government assistance Act in the US directs the treatment of creatures utilized in exploration, show, and business purposes, setting norms for their accommodating consideration and treatment.

IX. Continuous Difficulties and Contemporary Creature Government assistance Issues

The cutting edge creature government assistance development keeps on confronting various difficulties and face a scope of contemporary issues.

1. **Production line Cultivating and Modern Horticulture**

Industrial facility cultivating rehearses stay a combative issue, with worries about creature government assistance, ecological effect, and general wellbeing. Activists and associations are attempting to further develop conditions for livestock.

2. **Creature Testing and Exploration**

The utilization of creatures in logical exploration is a complex moral situation. Creature government assistance advocates push for the decrease, refinement, and supplanting of creature testing with elective strategies.

3. **Untamed life Preservation and Natural surroundings Insurance**

Natural life preservation endeavors are progressively basic even with territory misfortune, poaching, and environmental change. Advocates are battling for more grounded insurances for imperiled species and their biological systems.

4.3 Contemporary debates on animal personhood and legal rights

Whether or not creatures ought to be allowed legitimate personhood and privileges is at the front of contemporary moral and lawful discussions. While people have long depended on creatures for different purposes, like friendship, work, and food's, how society might interpret creatures' mental and close to home limits has developed altogether lately. This shift has prompted conversations about how we ought to treat creatures, according to an ethical viewpoint as well as from a lawful one. This paper investigates the contemporary discussions encompassing creature personhood and lawful freedoms, zeroing in on the contentions for and against perceiving creatures as legitimate people and stretching out legitimate privileges to them.

Authentic Viewpoint

From the beginning of time, creatures have been viewed as property, frequently utilized for human advantage without critical lawful insurance. Overall sets of laws have commonly classified creatures as things, regarding them as products instead of aware creatures with natural worth. The creature government assistance development, which started in the nineteenth hundred years, denoted a huge change in perspectives towards creatures, prompting the order of creature security regulations in numerous nations.

Be that as it may, notwithstanding these progressions, creatures are still prevalently treated as property in overall sets of laws around the world. Numerous creature advocates contend that this conventional view neglects to represent the complex mental and close to home existences of creatures and that the time has come to rethink the lawful status of creatures.

Contemporary Discussions
Creature Cognizance and Feeling

One of the essential contentions for allowing creatures legitimate personhood and freedoms is the developing collection of logical proof exhibiting that numerous creatures have mental and close to home limits that were recently misjudged or disregarded. Research in fields like ethology, mental science, and neurobiology has uncovered that creatures are fit for complex reasoning, encountering feelings, and showing social ways of behaving.

For instance, studies have shown that elephants display mindfulness, compassion, and long haul memory, while incredible gorillas, for example, chimpanzees and bonobos, display critical thinking abilities and social connections similar to human networks. Dolphins have shown progressed correspondence capacities and device use, while canines and felines display connection to their human guardians.

Recognizing these mental and profound capacities has incited the contention that creatures ought not be viewed as simple property yet rather creatures with characteristic worth meriting legitimate security. Advocates battle that the general set of laws ought to mirror our refreshed comprehension of creatures' capacities and requirements.

Lawful Privileges and Government assistance

Advocates for creature personhood contend that giving lawful freedoms to creatures is an important stage to shield them from different types of damage, including double-dealing, remorselessness, and disregard. Legitimate privileges would involve specific insurances and qualifications, like the right to life, freedom, and independence from pointless misery.

A few explicit legitimate freedoms that have been proposed for creatures incorporate the right to substantial honesty (security against mutilation or obtrusive methodology), the right to not be utilized in destructive logical examinations, and the option to live in a climate that considers regular ways of behaving. These privileges would lay out a benchmark of moral treatment and legitimate securities for creatures, intending to forestall savagery and double-dealing.

Preservation and Natural Worries

One more element of the creature personhood banter connects with protection and natural worries. Advocates contend that perceiving creatures as legitimate people and stretching out privileges to them can decidedly affect natural life and biological systems. Lawful personhood for creatures could prompt more grounded legitimate structures for the insurance of jeopardized species and their natural surroundings.

Besides, it could assist with laying out guardianship jobs for creatures, where people or associations are selected to act to the greatest advantage of creatures in judicial procedures. This approach could prompt more exhaustive and successful untamed life preservation endeavors and assist with alleviating the dangers of environment annihilation and environmental change.

The Resistance

While there is a developing development for creature personhood and lawful privileges, there are huge resistance and incredulity from different quarters. One of the primary worries raised by adversaries is the potential for antagonistic results to human interests and ventures. For instance, giving lawful personhood to animals could upset rehearses like processing plant cultivating, hunting, and creature trial and error, which are profoundly settled in numerous economies.

A few pundits contend that it very well might be illogical to give legitimate privileges to creatures, as it would make a lawful entanglement and essentially trouble the legal framework. Inquiries concerning how creatures would practice their freedoms and the ramifications for human-creature clashes are raised. Furthermore, there are worries that stretching out freedoms to creatures could prompt legitimate idiocies, like claims for creatures against their own hunters.

Rivals likewise feature that legitimate personhood and privileges for creatures might actually depreciate human existence and interests. They contend that perceiving creatures as legitimate people might obscure the differentiation among people and creatures, possibly subverting the moral and lawful groundworks of common freedoms.

Besides, a few pundits accept that working on creature government assistance through administrative measures and gradual changes is a more viable and powerful methodology. This point of view advocates for stricter creature government assistance regulations and guidelines as opposed to the expansive acknowledgment of lawful personhood.

Contemporary Models and Legitimate Turns of events

A few nations and locales have gained ground in perceiving creature personhood and stretching out lawful freedoms to creatures. Striking models include:

Non-Basic liberties Venture (NhRP) in the US: NhRP has been at the front of legitimate endeavors to get personhood and freedoms for specific non-human creatures, especially extraordinary chimps and elephants. Their work has prompted milestone legal disputes that stand out.

New Zealand's "Three Rs" Change: In 2015, New Zealand passed an alteration to its Creature Government assistance Act that perceived creatures as aware creatures and accentuated the significance of the "Three Rs": lessening, refining, and supplanting the utilization of creatures in research.

India's Acknowledgment of Dolphins as Non-Human People: In 2013, the Indian government formally acknowledged dolphins as non-human people, allowing them certain securities and privileges.

European Association's "Awareness Explanation": The European Association has perceived creatures as conscious creatures since the Deal of Amsterdam in 1997, recognizing their ability to encounter agony, enduring, and trouble.

These models show that the discussion over creature personhood and freedoms isn't just hypothetical however is common affecting general sets of laws and practices.

Chapter 5

The Ethics of Animal Use

The utilization of creatures by people is an unavoidable and complex moral issue that has produced broad discussions and conversations since the beginning of time. From horticulture and logical examination to diversion and friendship, people have used creatures for different purposes. This article dives into the morals of creature use, looking at the contentions for and against various types of creature abuse, the moral rules that support these contentions, and the advancing cultural perspectives towards creature use. To address this complex point sufficiently, we will investigate the morals of creature use in the accompanying settings: horticulture, logical exploration, diversion, and friendship.

1. Horticulture: The Usage of Creatures for Food and Items

Horticulture is one of the most far and wide and hostile types of creature use. The moral inquiries encompassing creature horticulture are well established in worries connected with creature government assistance, natural effect, and general wellbeing.

Moral Contentions For Creature Horticulture

1. **The Rule of Utilitarianism:** Utilitarian morals, which stresses augmenting generally speaking bliss and limiting anguish, can be utilized to contend that mindful and compassionate creature horticulture can give food and different items that add to human prosperity.

2. **Social and Monetary Significance:** Agribusiness including creatures frequently holds social importance, and it gives vocations to a huge number of individuals all over the planet. Advocates contend that it upholds rustic economies and customs.

3. **Moral Utilization:** A few defenders contend that consuming animal items from ranches that focus on animal government assistance, manageability, and compassionate practices can be morally reasonable.

Moral Contentions Against Creature Horticulture

1. **Animal Government assistance:** One of the most powerful cases against animal agribusiness is the huge enduring animals persevere in manufacturing plant cultivating, where conditions are frequently unforgiving, swarmed, and unsanitary. This raises worries about the intrinsic mercilessness of such practices.

2. **Ecological Effect:** The natural outcomes of creature farming, including deforestation, ozone harming substance discharges, and asset exhaustion, have raised moral worries about the manageability and long haul impacts of the business.

3. **Wellbeing Contemplations:** The utilization of creature items is related with different wellbeing gambles, including coronary illness and heftiness. Pundits contend that advancing plant-based slims down is all the more morally dependable.

II. Logical Exploration: Adjusting Progress and Moral Contemplations

Logical examination including creatures has been instrumental in propelling clinical information, drug advancement, and different fields. Be that as it may, it likewise raises significant moral quandaries.

Moral Contentions For Creature Exploration

1. **Clinical Advancement:** Defenders fight that numerous clinical leap forwards, like antibodies and medicines for sicknesses, could never have been conceivable without creature research. They contend that these advances benefit human wellbeing and save lives.

2. **Administrative Oversight:** Numerous nations have severe guidelines and moral rules set up to guarantee that creatures utilized in research are dealt with altruistically and with extreme attention to detail.

Moral Contentions Against Creature Exploration

1. **Creature Government assistance:** The essential moral concern encompassing creature research is the enduring of creatures included. Pundits contend that the damage incurred for creatures during tests is innately off-base and should be limited or wiped out.

2. **Elective Techniques:** Some contend that mechanical progressions have made it conceivable to foster options in contrast to creature research, for example, in vitro testing and PC demonstrating, which are more others conscious and possibly more powerful.

III. Diversion: Creatures in Carnivals, Zoos, and Game

Creatures have been utilized for diversion for a really long time, from bazaars and zoos to sports like horse racing and canine battling. This brings up significant moral issues about the treatment and imprisonment of creatures for human entertainment.

Moral Contentions For Creature Amusement

1. **Instruction and Protection:** A few defenders contend that zoos and aquariums fill instructive and preservation needs by bringing issues to light of imperiled species and their living spaces.
2. **Custom and Social Importance:** In certain societies, conventional works on including creatures are well established and thought about a fundamental piece of legacy and personality.

Moral Contentions Against Creature Diversion

1. **Creature Government assistance:** Pundits fight that many types of creature amusement include mercilessness, control, and constrained exhibitions, which hurt the prosperity of creatures.
2. **Moral Other options:** Advances in innovation and computer generated reality, as well as the advancement of brutality free diversion, have brought up issues about the need of involving creatures for entertainment.

IV. Friendship: Pets and Moral Obligation

The moral contemplations encompassing the utilization of creatures as pets envelop issues of creature government assistance, rearing practices, and dependable proprietorship.

Moral Contentions For Creature Friendship

1. **Bond and Prosperity:** Many individuals contend that having pets upgrades human prosperity through friendship, fondness, and consistent encouragement. They accept that creatures benefit from these connections too.
2. **Reception and Salvage:** A few backers advance taking on creatures from havens and salvages, as it gives homes to creatures out of luck and diminishes overbreeding.

Moral Contentions Against Creature Friendship

1. **Reproducing and Overpopulation:** Pundits contend that rearing practices, particularly those that focus on unambiguous attributes, can prompt overpopulation, medical problems, and experiencing in specific creature breeds.
2. **Obligation and Disregard:** The moral obligation of pet possession incorporates legitimate consideration, socialization, and consideration. Disregard, misuse, and surrender are viewed as serious moral infringement.

Changing Cultural Perspectives and Moral Advancement

Cultural perspectives towards the utilization of creatures have developed over the long haul, mirroring a developing familiarity with creature government assistance and moral worries. Propels in logical comprehension and changes in social standards have prompted expanded examination of practices that hurt creatures. Thus, there have been prominent changes in general assessment and legitimate changes focused on better

safeguarding creatures:

Legitimate Changes: Numerous nations have ordered regulations and guidelines to defend creature government assistance. These regulations envelop regions like creature remorselessness anticipation, imperiled species security, and limitations on creature use in examination and amusement.

Vegetarian and Plant-Based Developments: The ascent of veganism and plant-based eats less mirrors a change in customer inclinations toward more moral and practical food decisions. This has prompted the improvement of a scope of plant-based items and options in contrast to creature horticulture.

Moral Strategic policies: A few organizations are progressively taking on moral practices by carrying out creature government assistance guidelines and embracing mercilessness free standards. These organizations answer customer interest for additional others conscious and harmless to the ecosystem items.

Schooling and Support: Creature backing associations and developments play had a critical impact in bringing issues to light about the moral issues connected with creature use. They advance mindful decisions and urge individuals to think about the government assistance of creatures in their day to day routines.

5.1 The ethics of factory farming and industrial agriculture

Plant cultivating and modern agribusiness have become predominant frameworks of food creation in many areas of the planet, providing the developing worldwide interest for meat, dairy, and plant-based items. While these frameworks offer productivity and cost-viability, they likewise raise critical moral worries connected with creature government assistance, ecological manageability, and human wellbeing. This article analyzes the morals of manufacturing plant cultivating and modern horticulture, investigating the contentions for and against these practices and the moral rules that support these discussions. It additionally digs into the outcomes of these practices on creatures, the climate, and society, as well as expected answers for address the moral issues.

1. **Plant Cultivating: Moral Worries and Creature Government assistance**

Plant cultivating is portrayed by escalated and enormous scope domesticated animals creation, where creatures are brought up in restricted spaces and exposed to industrialized processes. The moral worries related with manufacturing plant cultivating basically spin around creature government assistance issues.

Moral Contentions For Processing plant Cultivating

1. **Proficiency and Cost-Viability:** Defenders contend that processing plant cultivating is more proficient as far as asset use and cost-viability, considering the creation of reasonable nourishment for a developing worldwide populace.

2. **Providing Worldwide Interest:** Manufacturing plant cultivating can fulfill the serious need for meat and creature based items, assisting with reducing food deficiencies and give protein-rich eating regimens.

Moral Contentions Against Processing plant Cultivating

1. **Animal Affliction:** One of the main moral worries is the broad enduring animals persevere in processing plant cultivating frameworks. Constrainment, congestion, mutilations, and stress-related medical problems are normal issues.
2. **Absence of Normal Ways of behaving:** Animals in plant cultivates frequently need some real open doors to communicate regular ways of behaving, like brushing, establishing, or mingling. This hardship brings up issues about the personal satisfaction for these creatures.
3. **Natural Effect:** The ecological outcomes of processing plant cultivating, including contamination from concentrated waste and ozone depleting substance discharges, raise moral worries about the effect on biological systems and people in the future.

II. Modern Horticulture: Moral Ramifications for the Climate

Modern farming alludes to enormous scope crop creation frameworks described by the weighty utilization of engineered inputs like composts and pesticides. The moral worries related with modern agribusiness are for the most part centered around ecological issues.

Moral Contentions For Modern Agribusiness

1. **Expanded Efficiency:** Defenders contend that modern horticulture considers higher harvest yields, empowering ranchers to create additional food from similar measure of land and assets.

2. **Taking care of a Developing Populace:** As the worldwide populace keeps on developing, modern farming is viewed as important to satisfy the rising need for food.

Moral Contentions Against Modern Farming

1. **Natural Debasement:** The inescapable utilization of engineered synthetic compounds and serious cultivating practices can prompt soil corruption, water contamination, and the deficiency of biodiversity. These outcomes present moral worries about the prosperity of the planet and people in the future.
2. **Wellbeing Suggestions:** The utilization of pesticides and composts can bring about tainting of food and water, presenting wellbeing dangers to the two buyers and farmworkers. This raises moral issues connected with general wellbeing and security.

III. Human Wellbeing and Food handling

Modern horticulture and processing plant cultivating have suggestions for human wellbeing and sanitation, prompting moral worries connected with the effect on individuals.

Moral Contentions For Modern Horticulture and Processing plant Cultivating

1. **Food Security:** Allies contend that these frameworks add to food security by delivering bigger amounts of food, which can assist with guaranteeing that individuals approach adequate and reasonable sustenance.
2. **Monetary Advantages:** The agrarian business gives work and financial open doors, especially in rustic regions. Advocates battle that these practices can invigorate financial development.

Moral Contentions Against Modern Horticulture and Industrial facility Cultivating

1. **Wellbeing Dangers:** The utilization of anti-infection agents and development chemicals in manufacturing plant cultivating can prompt wellbeing gambles, including anti-infection opposition and the presence of possibly hurtful deposits in food items.

2. **Specialist Double-dealing:** Farmworkers in modern agribusiness might confront troublesome working circumstances, low wages, and openness to destructive synthetic compounds, raising moral worries about work privileges and abuse.

3. **Influence on Weak People group:** These practices can excessively influence weak networks, for example, low-pay populaces and networks of variety, who might confront the brunt of ecological contamination and wellbeing gambles.

IV. Moral Standards Supporting the Discussions

The morals of manufacturing plant cultivating and modern horticulture are educated by different moral standards and philosophical structures:

Utilitarianism: Utilitarian morals, which accentuate augmenting generally speaking satisfaction and limiting affliction, can be utilized to contend both for and against production line cultivating and modern horticulture. Allies might contend that these frameworks give reasonable food to many, while pundits might zero in on the enduring of creatures, mischief to the climate, and wellbeing gambles.

Animal Government assistance Morals: Worries for animal government assistance support large numbers of the moral contentions against production line cultivating. This viewpoint underlines the need to lessen enduring and advance the prosperity of creatures.

Ecological Morals: Natural morals, which consider the moral and moral ramifications of human activities on the climate, drive a significant number of the moral worries connected with modern horticulture. It features the significance of reasonable and capable land and asset use.

General Wellbeing and Security: Moral standards connected with general wellbeing and security feature the significance of limiting dangers to human wellbeing, which can prompt reactions of modern agribusiness and plant cultivating rehearses.

V. Outcomes of Processing plant Cultivating and Modern Farming

The moral issues encompassing manufacturing plant cultivating and modern horticulture have genuine results that influence creatures, the climate, and society:

Animal Government assistance: Production line cultivating rehearses bring about broad languishing over creatures, including pressure, torment, and inconvenience. This effects the personal satisfaction for billions of creatures brought up in these frameworks.

Natural Debasement: Modern agribusiness adds to soil disintegration, water contamination, and environment obliteration, undermining biological systems and people in the future. It likewise compounds environmental change through ozone depleting substance discharges.

Human Wellbeing: The utilization of synthetics, anti-microbials, and chemicals in modern horticulture and plant cultivating can unfavorably affect general wellbeing, including anti-toxin opposition and openness to unsafe substances.

Work Issues: Laborers in these businesses might confront testing conditions, including low compensation, openness to risky substances, and lacking work freedoms.

VI. Possible Arrangements and Moral Reactions

Resolving the moral issues encompassing processing plant cultivating and modern farming requires a diverse methodology:

Maintainable Cultivating Works on: Progressing to additional reasonable and compassionate cultivating rehearses, for example, natural cultivating and field based creature farming, can diminish the negative ecological and animal government assistance influences.

Moral Utilization: Purchasers can pursue additional moral food decisions by supporting items from ranches and organizations that focus on animal government assistance, maintainability, and dependable agrarian practices.

Administrative Changes: Stricter guidelines and implementation can assist with lessening the adverse results of modern agribusiness and plant cultivating. This incorporates better oversight of synthetic use and creature government assistance norms.

Exploration and Development: Proceeded with investigation into elective rural techniques, like regenerative horticulture and vertical cultivating, can prompt more supportable and moral practices.

5.2 Animal testing and its moral implications

Creature testing, otherwise called creature trial and error or vivisection, is a broadly discussed practice in logical examination, clinical turn of events, and administrative testing. It includes involving creatures for examinations to propel human information and foster drugs, beauty care products, and different items. The ethical ramifications of creature testing have ignited extreme conversations and moral predicaments. On one hand, defenders contend that it is fundamental for logical advancement and human prosperity, while rivals raise serious moral worries about creature enduring, freedoms, and the improvement of elective techniques. This exposition inspects the ethical ramifications of creature testing, including contentions for and against the training, moral systems that support the discussion, and endeavors to find some kind of harmony between logical headway and creature government assistance.

1. **Contentions for Creature Testing**
   Logical Headways:
   One of the essential contentions for creature testing is its commitment to logical advancement and human prosperity. It is much of the time battled that without creature testing, numerous clinical leap forwards, including antibodies and medicines for sicknesses, could never have been conceivable. Creature models play had a pivotal impact in figuring out sickness systems and assessing the security and viability of likely therapies.
   Human Wellbeing and Security:
   Defenders contend that creature testing is fundamental for

guaranteeing the wellbeing and adequacy of drugs, clinical gadgets, and different items planned for human use. Testing on creatures is viewed as a basic move toward recognizing likely dangers and unfriendly impacts before these items are acquainted with the market or utilized on people.

Administrative Necessities:

Creature testing is frequently commanded by government organizations to meet administrative prerequisites for the endorsement of new medications, synthetics, and different substances. These organizations, like the U.S. Food and Medication Organization (FDA) and the European Meds Office (EMA), use information from creature testing to survey the wellbeing and adequacy of items.

Options Are Not Yet Adequate:

Defenders contend that while the improvement of elective techniques is progressing, they are not yet adequately progressed to supplant creature testing completely. In this way, creature models stay a vital part of logical examination and security testing.

2. **Contentions Against Creature Testing**

Creature Enduring and Government assistance:

The most convincing moral contention against creature testing spins around the broad affliction and mischief caused for creatures engaged with tests. Creatures are exposed to agony, stress, and enduring, frequently in cruel and unnatural conditions. Pundits contend that such damage is intrinsically off-base and raises serious moral worries.

Freedoms Based Morals:

A few rivals of creature testing contend from a rights-based moral point of view, fighting that creatures have characteristic worth and have specific freedoms, including the option to live without superfluous misery. They affirm that involving creatures as means to accomplish human finishes disregards these privileges.

Moral Other options:

Pundits underscore the advancement of elective strategies, for example, in vitro testing, PC displaying, and tissue designing, which can give more exact and accommodating ways of directing trials without utilizing creatures. These choices are viewed as morally predominant choices.

Absence of Translational Legitimacy:

A typical study of creature testing is its restricted translational legitimacy, implying that discoveries in creatures don't necessarily straightforwardly apply to people. Significant contrasts in physiology and science between species can prompt deluding results, possibly imperiling human wellbeing.

3. **Moral Systems in the Creature Testing Discussion**

Utilitarianism:

Utilitarian morals, which underscore expanding generally joy and limiting anguish, can be applied to the two sides of the creature testing banter. Advocates contend that creature testing benefits human prosperity, while rivals underline the experiencing persevered by creatures.

Creature Government assistance Morals:

The moral system of creature government assistance is established in the conviction that creatures ought to be treated with thought and gave a personal satisfaction that limits languishing. This structure illuminates numerous contentions against creature testing, as it features the damage caused for creatures engaged with tests.

Freedoms Based Morals:

A rights-based moral viewpoint states that creatures have intrinsic privileges, for example, the option to live liberated from pointless misery. This system supports numerous contentions against creature testing, as it fights that involving creatures as means to human closures is ethically unsuitable.

The Three Rs:

The Three Rs structure, which represents Substitution, Decrease, and Refinement, gives moral rules to creature testing. It advocates for the supplanting of creatures with elective strategies, the decrease of the quantity of creatures utilized, and the refinement of tests to limit languishing.

4. **Endeavors to Adjust Logical Headway and Creature Government assistance**

Perceiving the moral worries encompassing creature testing, there are continuous endeavors to find some kind of harmony between logical advancement and creature government assistance:

Improvement of Choices:

Critical exploration and venture have been coordinated towards the improvement of elective testing techniques that can give more exact and altruistic outcomes. These choices remember for vitro testing, PC displaying, and organ-on-a-chip innovation.

Moral Survey Sheets:

Many exploration foundations and colleges have laid out moral survey sheets to assess proposed creature tests. These sheets plan to guarantee that investigations are legitimate, refined to limit hurt, and steady with moral rules.

Reception of the Three Rs:

The Three Rs system has been generally embraced in established researchers, with an accentuation on supplanting creatures with choices, decreasing the quantity of creatures utilized, and refining trials to limit languishing.

Lawful and Administrative Changes:

A few nations have acquainted legitimate and administrative changes with diminish creature testing. For instance, the European Association has carried out limitations on creature testing for corrective items and fixings.

5.3 The ethics of using animals in entertainment and sports

The utilization of creatures in diversion and sports has a long history and keeps on being an exceptionally discussed moral issue. While creatures have been utilized for human entertainment in different structures, including bazaars, zoos, horse racing, canine battling, and marine parks, such practices raise significant moral worries about creature government assistance, freedoms, and our ethical constraints to non-human animals. This exposition digs into the morals of involving creatures in diversion and sports, investigating the contentions for and against these practices, the moral rules that support these discussions, and the advancing cultural mentalities towards the utilization of creatures for our amusement.

1. **The Utilization of Creatures in Diversion**
   Bazaars and Creature Exhibitions:
   Bazaars and creature exhibitions are the absolute most famous types of creature diversion. These shows frequently highlight creatures like elephants, large felines, and intriguing birds performing stunts for crowds. Defenders contend that these exhibitions offer instructive and amazing encounters.
   Zoos and Aquariums:
   Zoos and aquariums give potential chances to individuals to notice and find out about many creature species. Advocates contend that these organizations assume a urgent part in preservation endeavors and state funded training.
   Marine Parks and Dolphin Shows:
   Marine parks and dolphin shows are famous attractions that deal individuals the opportunity to see marine creatures like dolphins and executioner whales very close. Defenders guarantee that these encounters encourage a more profound appreciation for marine life.

2. **The Morals of Involving Creatures in Diversion**
   Creature Government assistance Concerns:
   One of the main moral worries is the potential for creature enduring and hurt for the sake of diversion. Creatures utilized in exhibitions frequently face conditions that might prompt pressure,

constrainment, and actual mischief. Pundits contend that these circumstances undermine their prosperity.

Privileges Based Morals:

A few rivals of creature diversion underscore privileges based moral points of view, contending that creatures have characteristic worth and certain freedoms, including the option to live liberated from superfluous misery. Involving creatures for our entertainment is viewed as an infringement of these freedoms.

Absence of Informed Assent:

Creatures utilized in amusement and sports don't give informed agree to partake. Pundits contend that this absence of assent brings up moral issues about independence and the treatment of conscious creatures.

Wellbeing Concerns:

The utilization of creatures in amusement can present dangers to the two creatures and people. Episodes including creatures getting away or harming mentors and observers have raised moral worries about the wellbeing of all included.

3. **The Utilization of Creatures in Sports**

Horse Racing:

Horse racing is a well known sport that includes pure blood ponies contending in races for prizes and magnificence. Advocates contend that the game is well established in custom and gives financial advantages to the business.

Greyhound Hustling:

Greyhound hustling is a type of canine dashing where greyhounds contend on tracks. Allies fight that the game is a chance for the creatures to practice and partake in their regular senses.

Creature Battling:

Creature battling incorporates bloodsports, for example, cockfighting and canine battling, where creatures are set in opposition to one another for diversion and betting. These practices are much of the time unlawful and broadly condemned on moral grounds.

4. **The Morals of Involving Creatures in Sports**

Creature Government assistance and Abuse:

Quite possibly of the most convincing moral worry in creature sports is the potential for damage and abuse. Creatures in these games might be exposed to brutal preparation strategies, actual wounds, and even demise. Pundits contend that such practices abuse creature government assistance standards.

Moral Other options:

Rivals of creature sports feature that moral options exist, for example, human-just games and computer experiences, which kill the need to take advantage of creatures for our amusement.

Spectatorship and Public Discernment:

The morals of creature sports are additionally connected with the ethical obligation of onlookers. Joining in or supporting such occasions might add to the propagation of creature double-dealing and enduring, bringing up issues about the moral commitments of the crowd.

5. **Moral Structures in the Utilization of Creatures for Diversion and Sports**

Creature Government assistance Morals:

Creature government assistance morals focus on the prosperity and sympathetic treatment of creatures. Worries for creature government assistance support numerous contentions against the utilization of creatures in amusement and sports, accentuating the likely torment and mischief included.

Privileges Based Morals:

A rights-based moral point of view declares that creatures have intrinsic privileges, including the option to live liberated from superfluous misery and double-dealing. This structure illuminates contentions against creature diversion and sports.

Utilitarianism:

Utilitarian morals, which underscore expanding by and large joy and limiting misery, can be utilized to contend both for and against the utilization of creatures in amusement and sports. Defenders might contend that these practices give satisfaction to people, while pundits center around the experiencing persevered by creatures.

Natural Morals:

Natural morals, which think about the ethical ramifications of human activities on the climate, illuminate the discussion on involving creatures in amusement. This structure brings up issues about the effect of such practices on the environments and territories of these creatures.

6. **Changing Cultural Perspectives and Moral Advancement**

Cultural mentalities towards the utilization of creatures in diversion and sports have developed after some time. Expanding attention to creature government assistance and moral contemplations has prompted massive changes and progress:

Lawful Changes:

Numerous nations have carried out lawful changes to safeguard creatures utilized in amusement and sports. These changes frequently remember guidelines for creature government assistance, security measures, and prohibitions on specific practices like creature battling.

Moral Other options:

The advancement of moral other options, for example, creature free bazaars, natural life asylums, and altruistic equestrian occasions, offers more moral choices for amusement and sports devotees.

Public Mindfulness:

Creature government assistance associations and promotion endeavors play had a huge impact in bringing issues to light about the moral worries connected with creature diversion and sports. Public mindfulness and changing mentalities have prompted a decrease in participation at certain occasions and a shift towards additional moral practices.

Corporate Obligation:

Organizations and associations have likewise done whatever it may take to embrace more moral practices in diversion and sports. For instance, a few carriers have quit moving creatures for carnivals, and scenes have eliminated creature exhibitions in light of public worries.

Chapter 6

Conservation and Biodiversity

Preservation and biodiversity are two interrelated ideas that assume an essential part in supporting life on The planet. Biodiversity, frequently alluded to as the assortment of life, envelops the variety of species, biological systems, and hereditary variety inside species. Preservation, then again, is the conscious and reasonable administration of normal assets to guarantee their drawn out feasibility. In this extensive investigation, we will dive into the meaning of biodiversity, the ongoing dangers it faces, and the systems and practices utilized in protection endeavors.

The Significance of Biodiversity

Biodiversity is the groundwork of life on The planet and gives a huge number of biological system administrations fundamental for human prosperity. One of its essential capabilities is keeping up with biological system soundness and flexibility. Various biological systems are better prepared to endure natural changes, adjust to aggravations, and recuperate from debacles. This versatility is pivotal for guaranteeing the security of administrations like fertilization, water sanitization, and environment guideline.

Besides, biodiversity adds to human government assistance in different ways, including the arrangement of food, medication, and unrefined components. Large numbers of the harvests we depend on for food and the drugs that treat infections are gotten from different plant and creature species. Biodiversity likewise assumes a basic part in social and sporting exercises, molding customs, old stories, and the travel industry.

Dangers to Biodiversity

Regardless of its basic significance, biodiversity is confronting remarkable dangers, fundamentally determined by human exercises. Environment obliteration and discontinuity, driven by urbanization, horticulture, and foundation advancement, are significant supporters of the deficiency of biodiversity. As regular living spaces vanish, species lose their homes and battle to get by.

Environmental change, an outcome of human-incited exercises like consuming non-renewable energy sources, deforestation, and modern cycles, represents another critical danger. Adjusted temperature designs, outrageous climate occasions, and moving precipitation designs disturb environments and effect species appropriations, in some cases prompting the annihilation of weak populaces.

Overexploitation of regular assets, for example, overfishing and poaching, is an immediate result of unreasonable human utilization designs. This exhausts populaces of target species as well as disturbs the equilibrium of whole biological systems. Contamination, including air, water, and soil contamination, further mixtures the difficulties looked by biodiversity, prompting the downfall of species and the corruption of environments.

Preservation Techniques and Practices

Given the criticalness of the biodiversity emergency, preservation techniques and practices have become principal. One essential methodology is the foundation and the executives of safeguarded regions. Public parks, untamed life safe-havens, and marine stores go about as sanctuaries for biodiversity, giving places of refuge where biological systems can flourish undisturbed. Furthermore, these regions act as places for logical examination and schooling.

Living space reclamation is another key protection practice. Endeavors to restore debased biological systems, replant local vegetation, and once again introduce species into their normal territories can assist with switching a portion of the harm brought about by human exercises. This approach requires cautious preparation and checking to guarantee the progress of reclamation projects.

Protection hereditary qualities assumes a pivotal part in keeping up with hereditary variety inside species. By understanding the hereditary cosmetics of populaces, preservationists can execute systems to forestall inbreeding and keep up with sound genetic stocks. This is especially significant for imperiled species with little, confined populaces.

Local area based protection approaches include nearby networks in the preservation cycle. Perceiving the significance of customary information and including nearby occupants in dynamic makes a feeling of pride and guarantees the economical utilization of regular assets. This approach additionally frequently prompts more powerful and socially touchy protection drives.

Feasible asset the board is a foundation of preservation endeavors. This includes taking on rehearses that consider the utilization of regular assets without undermining their drawn out practicality. For instance, maintainable ranger service rehearses guarantee the proceeded with strength of timberlands, while mindful fisheries the executives means to forestall overfishing and safeguard marine environments.

Preservation Examples of overcoming adversity

While the difficulties to biodiversity are huge, there have been outstanding triumphs in protection endeavors. One such example of overcoming adversity is the recuperation of specific species from the verge of annihilation. The bald eagle, for example, confronted an extreme populace decline because of the utilization of the pesticide DDT. Through coordinated preservation endeavors, remembering the boycott for DDT and territory security, the bald eagle populace bounced back, and it was eliminated from the jeopardized species list in 2007.

One more example of overcoming adversity is the protection of the monster panda in China. Confronting natural surroundings misfortune and a declining bamboo supply, monster pandas were very nearly eradication. China executed a complete preservation program that included environment insurance, hostage rearing, and local area inclusion. Accordingly, the monster panda populace has expanded, and it was minimized from imperiled to weak on the Global Association for Protection of Nature (IUCN) Red Rundown.

Difficulties and Future Headings

Regardless of these examples of overcoming adversity, critical difficulties endure in the domain of biodiversity protection. One significant obstruction is the absence of mindfulness and understanding among the overall population in regards to the significance of biodiversity and the dangers it faces. Training and effort programs are crucial for overcome this issue and encourage a more noteworthy feeling of natural obligation.

Worldwide coordination is another test, as numerous species move across borders and are dependent upon global exchange. Executing powerful preservation methodologies requires joint effort between nations, associations, and networks. Moreover, tending to the main drivers of biodiversity misfortune, for example, impractical utilization designs and monetary frameworks that focus on momentary increases over long haul manageability, is critical for accomplishing significant and enduring protection results.

The coordination of innovation into protection endeavors presents the two open doors and difficulties. High level apparatuses like remote detecting, DNA examination, and man-made consciousness can upgrade checking and research capacities. In any case, the moral ramifications of advances like quality altering and geoengineering need cautious thought to guarantee that mediations don't have potentially negative results on environments.

Despite these difficulties, there is a developing acknowledgment of the requirement for groundbreaking change in the manner society connects with the climate. This incorporates rethinking our utilization designs, progressing to practical energy sources, and integrating natural contemplations into dynamic cycles at all levels.

6.1 The ethical considerations of conserving endangered species

The preservation of imperiled species is a mind boggling and diverse undertaking that goes past logical and biological aspects. At its center, the preservation of imperiled species includes moral contemplations that gauge the benefit of saving biodiversity against contending human interests. In this investigation, we dig into the moral elements of moderating imperiled species, looking at the ethical constraints, clashing qualities, and the fragile harmony between human necessities and the characteristic worth of every living being.

The Characteristic Worth of Species

One of the essential moral contemplations in preserving jeopardized species lies in perceiving the natural worth of every species. The inborn worth contention attests that species have intrinsic worth, autonomous of their utility to people. This point of view difficulties anthropocentrism — the view that main human interests have characteristic worth — and underlines the significance of safeguarding the variety of life for the good of its own.

From a moral stance, every species adds to the extravagance and intricacy of biological systems, and their reality has tasteful, social, and otherworldly importance. The eradication of an animal categories implies the irreversible loss of a novel arrangement of qualities, ways of behaving, and biological jobs. Preservation endeavors grounded in the natural worth point of view mean to safeguard species for their reality, recognizing that each specie has an option to endure on The planet.

Human-centric Qualities and Utilitarianism

Nonetheless, moral contemplations in preservation frequently meet with human interests and needs. Human-centric qualities, which focus on human prosperity and success, some of the time struggle with the safeguarding of imperiled species. Utilitarian contentions might emerge, recommending that preservation endeavors ought to be legitimate in light of the best really great for the best number of individuals.

In this specific situation, moral problems arise, driving society to adjust the characteristic worth of species against financial turn of events, asset extraction, and land use. The moral test lies in tracking down an agreeable concurrence between human exercises and the safeguarding of biodiversity, staying away from a utilitarian methodology that forfeits the prosperity of species for momentary human increases.

Honest convictions and Stewardship

A moral structure for protection frequently includes a feeling of ethical commitment and stewardship towards the planet and its occupants. The idea of stewardship stresses mankind's liability to really focus on and safeguard the regular world.

This ethical obligation stretches out to people in the future, as choices made today with respect to the preservation of imperiled species significantly influence the prosperity of those on the way.

Recognizing this ethical commitment requires a change in context, creating some distance from review nature as an asset to be taken advantage of and remembering it as a perplexing snare of life that requests our regard and security. The inquiry then becomes: What moral obligations do we have as stewards of the Earth, and how do these obligations direct our activities in monitoring jeopardized species?

Moral Problems in Protection Practices

Preservation rehearses themselves frequently present moral quandaries. For instance, hostage reproducing programs are regularly utilized to help the populaces of jeopardized species. While these projects can be instrumental in forestalling annihilation, concerns emerge about the moral treatment of individual creatures in imprisonment. Inquiries concerning the prosperity, mental wellbeing, and the potential for renewed introduction into the wild should be painstakingly thought of.

Essentially, natural surroundings reclamation endeavors might include uprooting human networks or adjusting scenes, bringing up issues about ecological equity and the privileges of nearby populaces. Finding some kind of harmony between the moral treatment of the two people and non-human species turns into a complicated test chasing preservation objectives.

Hereditary designing and de-elimination advancements likewise present moral contemplations. While these advances might offer imaginative answers for resuscitate wiped out species or upgrade the hereditary variety of imperiled populaces, moral inquiries concerning playing "nature's job" and the potentially negative results of controlling environments should be entirely tended to.

Interconnectedness of Moral Contemplations

The moral contemplations of moderating imperiled species are interconnected and require a comprehensive methodology. For example, the moral treatment of creatures in preservation rehearses ties straightforwardly to the natural worth contention, accentuating the significance of regarding the respect and prosperity of individual animals. The utilitarian viewpoint crosses with human-centric qualities, encouraging a cautious assessment of the outcomes of preservation choices on human social orders.

Besides, the interconnectedness reaches out to worldwide moral contemplations, as protection endeavors frequently rise above political boundaries. Cooperative global drives are important to address the transboundary idea of biodiversity and advance a common moral obligation regarding the conservation of species around the world.

Native Points of view and Conventional Information

A moral investigation of preservation should incorporate native points of view and conventional information. Native people group frequently have special associations with their surroundings and have exceptionally old insight about manageable concurrence with nature. Perceiving and regarding native freedoms and information frameworks is critical for moral preservation rehearses.

Native people group might see the protection of specific species as vital to their social personality and otherworldliness. Moral contemplations, thusly, reach out past the organic domain to incorporate social and common liberties aspects. Cooperative preservation endeavors that include and regard native viewpoints add to both biodiversity protection and moral obligation.

Instruction and Moral Mindfulness

Tending to the moral components of saving imperiled species requires a far reaching comprehension of the significance of biodiversity and the moral ramifications of human activities. Instructive projects assume a vital part in bringing issues to light about the natural worth of species, the interconnectedness of environments, and the moral obligations of people and social orders.

Advancing moral mindfulness likewise includes encouraging a feeling of sympathy towards different species. Figuring out the mind boggling ways of behaving, social designs, and close to home limits of imperiled species can inspire a more profound moral association and a more noteworthy obligation to their preservation.

6.2 Balancing the needs of humans and animals in conservation efforts

Protection endeavors wrestle with a sensitive difficult exercise between the requirements of people and the conservation of creature species and their environments. The perplexing transaction between ecological manageability, monetary turn of events, and civil rights highlights the difficulties of tracking down an amicable conjunction. In this investigation, we dig into the diverse elements of this equilibrium, analyzing the moral contemplations, financial variables, and imaginative methodologies that add to powerful protection while tending to the authentic requirements of human networks.

The Interconnectedness of Human and Creature Prosperity

Understanding the many-sided association between human prosperity and the wellbeing of environments is fundamental to accomplishing a feasible equilibrium. Biological system administrations, like clean water, fertilization, and environment guideline, straightforwardly influence human endurance and success.

All the while, the preservation of biodiversity is pivotal for keeping up with the natural cycles that support life on The planet.

Moderating creature species frequently includes protecting their environments, which can conflict with human exercises like farming, foundation improvement, and urbanization. Perceiving the interconnectedness of human and creature prosperity stresses that the preservation of one is personally attached to the government assistance of the other. A decent methodology, subsequently, looks for arrangements that encourage conjunction instead of conflict.

Moral Contemplations in Human-Creature Equilibrium

Moral contemplations assume a urgent part in exploring the intricacies of adjusting human necessities and creature protection. Regard for the natural worth of both human and non-human existence requires a cautious assessment of the results of preservation activities on neighborhood networks and untamed life.

From a moral viewpoint, recognizing the privileges of native networks and customary social orders that exist together with wildlife is fundamental. Regard for social variety and the combination of customary information into protection rehearses add to moral and successful arrangements. Moral contemplations likewise stretch out to the sympathetic treatment of creatures in protection endeavors, for example, limiting pressure during research and guaranteeing the prosperity of creatures in bondage or under restoration.

Adjusting the necessities of people and creatures requires moral structures that address inquiries of equity, reasonableness, and the impartial dissemination of the two advantages and weights related with protection activities. Finding some kind of harmony involves perceiving that preservation shouldn't lopsidedly trouble underestimated networks or undermine their jobs.

Financial Effects of Protection

Preservation drives can monetarily affect neighborhood networks, frequently making strains between the basic to safeguard untamed life and the requirement for financial turn of events. For instance, the foundation of safeguarded regions might prompt the dislodging of native populaces or limitations on conventional land use. Understanding and moderating these financial effects are basic for accomplishing an equilibrium that regards both human and creature needs.

The deficiency of jobs, especially in networks reliant upon normal assets, can bring about disdain towards protection endeavors. This highlights the significance of incorporating social contemplations into preservation arranging, guaranteeing that financial other options and reasonable practices are carried out to counterbalance the expected adverse consequences on nearby networks.

Imaginative methodologies, for example, local area based protection, engage nearby inhabitants to become stewards of their surroundings. By including networks in dynamic cycles and giving monetary impetuses to protection, adjusting human necessities to the conservation of biodiversity is conceivable.

Feasible Asset The board

A vital part of accomplishing balance lies in feasible asset the board. The overexploitation of regular assets, driven by impractical practices, represents a huge danger to both human and creature prosperity. Embracing reasonable asset the board rehearses guarantees that environments can keep on offering fundamental types of assistance while addressing the requirements of human networks.

With regards to fisheries, for example, carrying out maintainable reaping works on, directing fishing portions, and laying out marine safeguarded regions add to the preservation of marine biodiversity while taking into account the proceeded with livelihoods of fishing networks. Also, feasible ranger service rehearses advance the drawn out strength of backwoods and the protection of species subject to these biological systems.

Compromise Methodologies

In locales where human and untamed life clashes are pervasive, it is central to track down compelling compromise systems. Rivalry for assets, especially in regions where farming infringes upon normal living spaces, can prompt negative communications among people and animals. Carrying out measures like untamed life halls, secure fencing, and local area driven compromise drives lessens pressures and encourages concurrence.

In situations where huge carnivores, similar to lions or panthers, represent a danger to animals and human wellbeing, utilizing non-deadly strategies, like secure nooks and sound impediments, can safeguard the two people and creatures. It is fundamental to perceive that clashes are frequently suggestive of more extensive issues, like destitution or absence of elective vocations, and addressing these main drivers is vital to feasible compromise.

Imaginative Preservation Approaches

Development assumes a vital part in tracking down arrangements that balance human and creature needs. Mechanical headways, for example, geospatial planning and remote detecting, help in recognizing areas of high preservation need while limiting adverse consequences on human exercises. These apparatuses improve the accuracy of protection arranging, taking into consideration more educated navigation.

Besides, the combination of ecotourism gives a reasonable monetary elective that adjusts preservation to the interests of neighborhood networks. When overseen dependably, ecotourism can produce pay, make occupations, and bring issues to light about the benefit of protecting regular territories and the species they support.

The idea of "Installments for Environment Administrations" (PES) is one more imaginative methodology that perceives the worth of biological system benefits and remunerates networks for their job in protection. This component upholds the conservation of biodiversity as well as recognizes the commitments of neighborhood networks in keeping up with solid biological systems.

Schooling and Local area Commitment

Training and local area commitment are urgent parts of accomplishing a harmony among human and creature needs in preservation endeavors. Bringing issues to light about the significance of biodiversity, the natural administrations given by solid environments, and the worth of conjunction cultivates a feeling of shared liability.

Local area based preservation drives that include nearby occupants in dynamic cycles enable networks to take responsibility for endeavors. This cooperative methodology guarantees that protection techniques are socially touchy, monetarily practical, and lined up with the requirements and goals of individuals straightforwardly influenced by these endeavors.

6.3 The role of zoos and sanctuaries in animal conservation

Zoos and safe-havens assume a critical part in the perplexing scene of creature protection. While their missions and strategies might vary, the two establishments add to the safeguarding of biodiversity, instruction, research, and the government assistance of individual creatures. In this investigation, we dive into the multi-layered jobs of zoos and safe-havens in creature protection, looking at their particular commitments, moral contemplations, and the developing idea of their parts in an impacting world.

Zoos as Protection Establishments

Zoos have gone through a groundbreaking development from simple diversion settings to imperative supporters of worldwide protection endeavors. Current zoos presently focus on preservation, instruction, examination, and creature government assistance as center parts of their central goal.

Preservation Reproducing Projects: Zoos are effectively associated with protection rearing projects, especially for imperiled species confronting the danger of elimination. By keeping up with hereditarily different populaces of imperiled creatures, zoos go about as arks, protecting species from the edge of elimination. Models incorporate the fruitful reproducing programs for the California condor and the Amur panther.

Ex Situ Protection: Zoos participate in ex situ preservation, which includes the upkeep of species outside their normal territories. While pundits contend that creatures ought to be in the wild, ex situ protection fills in as a significant insurance contract against horrendous occasions like catastrophic events, illnesses, or natural surroundings obliteration. Zoos frequently team up with administrative and non-legislative associations to once again introduce hostage reared people into nature.

State funded Instruction and Mindfulness: Zoos act as strong instructive stages, furnishing guests with bits of knowledge into the normal world and the significance of biodiversity. Through interpretive displays, instructive projects, and intuitive encounters, zoos bring issues to light about preservation issues and motivate a feeling of stewardship among the general population.

Moral Contemplations in Zoos

While zoos contribute fundamentally to protection, moral worries encompass their reality, especially connected with creature government assistance, imprisonment, and the accentuation on specific appealling species over others.

Creature Government assistance: Guaranteeing the prosperity of creatures in bondage is an essential moral concern. Present day zoos endeavor to establish conditions that imitate normal territories, give mental and actual excitement, and focus on the wellbeing and solace of the creatures. Moral zoos put resources into improvement programs, veterinary consideration, and extensive walled in areas to upgrade the personal satisfaction for their occupants.

Training versus Diversion: Finding some kind of harmony between instructive goals and amusement esteem is quite difficult for zoos. Moral zoos focus on instructive substance, preservation informing, and the advancement of sympathy and regard for creatures over shocking shows planned exclusively for amusement.

Specific Reproducing: The particular rearing of specific alluring species for preservation purposes can prompt the disregard of less well known however biologically urgent species. Moral contemplations incorporate guaranteeing that protection endeavors are adjusted and include many species, in addition to those that catch public consideration.

Safe-havens as Shelters for Saved Creatures

Safe-havens, as opposed to zoos, frequently center around giving a shelter to protected creatures that have been uprooted, mishandled, or resigned from different circumstances. Their essential mission is revolved around creature government assistance, recovery, and offering a long lasting home for creatures out of luck.

Salvage and Recovery: Safe-havens salvage creatures from different circumstances, including unlawful natural life exchange, carnivals, side of the road attractions, and confidential proprietorship. These creatures might have physical or mental injury, and safe-havens focus on their restoration, giving a protected and naturalistic climate where they can recuperate.

Lifetime Care: Asylums focus on giving lifetime care to their inhabitants. Not at all like zoos, which might have reproducing projects and spotlight on unambiguous species, safe-havens frequently have a different scope of creatures, including those that may not be reasonable for renewed introduction into the wild because of physical or conduct difficulties.

Schooling and Promotion: While safe-havens are principally centered around the government assistance of individual creatures, many likewise participate in training and backing endeavors. Through directed visits, instructive projects, and effort drives, asylums plan to bring issues to light about the predicament of creatures in imprisonment and the significance of moral treatment.

Moral Contemplations in Safe-havens

Safe-havens are by and large apparent as more morally lined up with creature government assistance, however they additionally face difficulties and moral contemplations.

Monetary Maintainability: Safe-havens frequently depend on open help and gifts, and monetary manageability can be a critical test. Keeping up with exclusive expectations of care, including veterinary administrations, legitimate sustenance, and open nooks, requires a consistent wellspring of subsidizing.

Species-Explicit Necessities: Accommodating the different necessities of various species, particularly those with complex social designs or explicit environment prerequisites, is a consistent moral thought. Asylums should guarantee that their offices are prepared to meet the physical, mental, and social requirements of the creatures under their consideration.

No Reproducing Strategies: Numerous respectable safe-havens stick to a severe "no rearing" strategy to try not to add to the excess of hostage creatures. This strategy lines up with a moral position that focuses on the government assistance of individual creatures over the protection objectives related with rearing projects in zoos.

Coordinated efforts and Developing Jobs

As of late, there has been a developing acknowledgment of the correlative jobs that zoos and safe-havens can play in the more extensive scene of creature preservation.

Cooperative Protection Drives: Zoos and safe-havens progressively team up on preservation drives. Zoos might uphold asylums in saving and really focusing on creatures, while safe-havens add to instructive and mindfulness programs drove by zoos. Such coordinated efforts upgrade the general effect of protection endeavors.

Research Associations: The two zoos and safe-havens participate in logical examination to add to how we might interpret creature conduct, wellbeing, and protection science. Cooperative exploration drives between these establishments and scholarly associations further fortify the logical premise of protection rehearses.

Support for Moral Practices: Zoos and safe-havens the same have become advocates for moral practices inside the more extensive domain of creature care. This incorporates pushing for regulation that controls the confidential responsibility for creatures, disallowing specific awful practices, and advancing the best expectations of creature government assistance.

The Eventual fate of Zoos and Safe-havens in Creature Protection

The fate of zoos and asylums in creature preservation will probably be formed by progressing endeavors to address moral worries, advance logical exploration, and adjust to changing cultural perspectives.

Proceeded with Accentuation on Protection: Zoos will probably proceed with their shift toward a more grounded accentuation on preservation, training, and examination. This development lines up with a more extensive cultural consciousness of ecological issues and the requirement for coordinated endeavors to address biodiversity misfortune.

Improved Creature Government assistance Guidelines: The two zoos and safe-havens will probably confront expanding strain to upgrade creature government assistance norms. The public's assumptions about the moral treatment of creatures in bondage are developing, prompting a more prominent accentuation on roomy nooks, naturalistic conditions, and enhancement programs.

Training as a Main thrust: The instructive job of zoos and safe-havens is probably going to turn out to be considerably more basic. As open familiarity with preservation issues keeps on rising, these foundations will assume a fundamental part in rousing people to pursue informed decisions that add to the prosperity of creatures and the planet.

Mechanical Developments: Progressions in innovation, for example, augmented reality encounters and live-streaming, may offer new roads for zoos and safe-havens to draw in with general society. This could improve instructive effort and give experiences into the existences of creatures such that regards their government assistance.

Chapter 7

Ethical Consumerism and Animal Welfare

Moral commercialization, the cognizant and conscious decision to buy items that line up with one's qualities and moral convictions, has turned into a strong power in molding markets and impacting corporate practices. Inside the domain of moral industrialism, the treatment of animals is a focal concern, incorporating issues, for example, plant cultivating, creature testing, and manageable practices. In this far reaching investigation, we dive into the multifaceted connection between moral commercialization and creature government assistance, analyzing the moral contemplations, the effect of customer decisions, and the potential for positive change in advancing the prosperity of creatures through careful utilization.

The Groundworks of Moral Industrialism

1.1 Characterizing Moral Industrialism:

Moral commercialization is established in the possibility that purchasers have the ability to impact strategic policies by settling on informed decisions lined up with their qualities. This idea incorporates a great many moral contemplations, including ecological manageability, fair work practices, and creature government assistance. With regards to creature government assistance, moral commercialization includes settling on decisions that mirror a promise to the sympathetic treatment of creatures in different ventures.

1.2 The Ascent of Cognizant Commercialization:

The shift towards cognizant commercialization has picked up speed in light of developing consciousness of social and natural issues. Shoppers are progressively looking for straightforwardness, responsibility, and moral practices from organizations. As worries about creature government assistance become more unmistakable, people are utilizing their buying ability to help items and organizations that focus on accommodating treatment of creatures.

1.3 The Job of Values in Customer Decisions:

Customer decisions are much of the time driven by private qualities, convictions, and moral contemplations. Understanding the inspirations driving moral industrialism is pivotal for appreciating how people explore the perplexing scene of buying choices concerning creature government assistance.

Values like sympathy, ecological stewardship, and civil rights assume a significant part in forming the moral customer's outlook.

Creature Government assistance in Shopper Decisions

2.1 Processing plant Cultivating and Choices:

One of the focal issues inside the domain of animal government assistance is the effect of industrial facility cultivating on creatures. Moral buyers frequently look for options in contrast to expectedly created meat, dairy, and eggs. This part investigates the moral worries related with processing plant cultivating works on, including stuffed conditions, utilization of anti-infection agents, and the ecological effect. It likewise digs into the ascent of elective choices, for example, plant-based abstains from food, natural cultivating, and free roaming creature farming.

2.2 Creature Testing and Brutality Free Items:

The corrective and drug businesses have for quite some time been censured for exposing creatures to testing strategies. Moral customers advocate for savagery free items, inciting the improvement of choices and a shift towards more compassionate testing strategies. This segment looks at the moral problems related with creature testing, the development of remorselessness free accreditations, and the job of buyers in driving change through their buying decisions.

2.3 Supportable Fish Practices:

Overfishing and horrendous fishing rehearses have raised worries about the exhaustion of marine environments and the government assistance of amphibian species. Moral customers are progressively centered around supporting economical fish rehearses that focus on capable fishing, safeguard marine biodiversity, and try not to add to issues like bycatch and environment obliteration. This part investigates the difficulties and progress in advancing moral decisions in fish utilization.

The Effect of Moral Commercialization on Businesses

3.1 Changing Rural Practices:

The interest for morally created food has impacted horticultural works on, prompting a reconsideration of conventional cultivating strategies. Natural cultivating, field raised domesticated animals, and agroecological approaches have built up forward momentum as customers look for items that line up with their qualities. This part inspects the extraordinary effect of moral industrialism on the farming business and the difficulties and potential open doors related with these movements.

3.2 Restorative and Style Enterprises:

The excellence and mold enterprises have seen a change in perspective driven by moral commercialization. Mercilessness free magnificence items and maintainable design rehearses are turning out to be progressively well known, mirroring a developing familiarity with the moral ramifications of these enterprises. This part investigates the developing scene of moral decisions in beauty care products and design, resolving issues, for example, fur cultivating, calfskin creation, and eco-accommodating other options.

3.3 Ascent of Plant-Based and Elective Items:

The flood popular for plant-based and elective items is reshaping the food business. Moral purchasers, persuaded by worries about creature government assistance, natural maintainability, and wellbeing, are driving the development of plant-based diets and meat substitutes. This segment investigates the expanding market for plant-based food sources, the developments in elective protein sources, and the more extensive ramifications for the food business.

Difficulties and Reactions of Moral Commercialization

4.1 Greenwashing and Moral Worries:

As moral industrialism acquires ubiquity, worries about greenwashing — where organizations misrepresent or dishonestly guarantee their moral practices — have arisen. This segment digs into the difficulties of exploring a commercial center soaked with moral cases, the significance of straightforwardness, and the requirement for dependable confirmations to direct customer decisions.

4.2 Availability and Reasonableness:

A typical analysis of moral commercialization is its apparent elitism. Practical and morally delivered items are frequently connected with greater cost places, restricting openness for certain buyers. This segment investigates the difficulties of pursuing moral decisions more comprehensive, resolving issues of moderateness, and looking at drives pointed toward democratizing moral utilization.

4.3 Adjusting Moral Needs:

Shoppers frequently face complex moral decisions where contending needs should be gauged. For example, the ecological effect of specific plant-based items, transportation contemplations, or the monetary prosperity of neighborhood ranchers. This part looks at the difficulties of adjusting numerous moral contemplations and the significance of nuanced dynamic in the domain of moral commercialization.

The Fate of Moral Commercialization and Creature Government assistance

5.1 Innovation and Straightforwardness:

Progressions in innovation, for example, blockchain and store network straightforwardness devices, hold the possibility to upset how buyers access data about the items they buy. This segment investigates the job of innovation in upgrading straightforwardness, decreasing data lopsidedness, and engaging customers to pursue more educated moral decisions.

5.2 Instructive Drives and Mindfulness:

Instructive missions and drives assume a pivotal part in forming buyer mindfulness and conduct. This part investigates the effect of instructive projects, advertising efforts, and grassroots developments in bringing issues to light about creature government assistance issues, encouraging moral commercialization, and driving positive change.

5.3 Strategy and Guideline:

The job of government strategies and guidelines in advancing creature government assistance and moral commercialization is huge. This part looks at the potential for administrative systems to boost moral practices, guarantee the exactness of item naming, and make a level battleground that upholds organizations focused on high moral principles.

5.4 Worldwide Coordinated effort:

As moral industrialism rises above public lines, worldwide cooperation is progressively imperative. Worldwide drives, associations between states, organizations, and non-legislative associations can enhance the effect of moral commercialization on a worldwide scale. This part investigates the potential for cooperative endeavors to address complex difficulties and advance creature government assistance around the world.

7.1 Making ethical choices in food and product consumption

In the cutting edge period, moral decisions in food and item utilization have arisen as a strong means for people to communicate their qualities and add to an additional sympathetic and supportable world. From the food on our plates to the items we utilize everyday, purchasers presently can pursue informed choices that line up with moral contemplations like creature government assistance, ecological manageability, and fair work rehearses. In this investigation, we dive into the standards of moral utilization, the effect of our decisions, and commonsense procedures for exploring the perplexing scene of moral navigation.

Grasping Moral Utilization

1.1 Characterizing Moral Utilization:

Moral utilization includes settling on cognizant and conscious decisions that focus on values like reasonableness, supportability, and sympathy. This reaches out across different parts of utilization, including food, clothing, individual consideration items, and family things. Understanding the interconnectedness of these decisions is critical for building a comprehensive way to deal with moral living.

1.2 Standards of Moral Utilization:

The rules that guide moral utilization incorporate a scope of contemplations, including:

Animal Government assistance: Picking items that maintain compassionate treatment of animals, staying away from those related with manufacturing plant cultivating, creature testing, or different types of double-dealing.

Ecological Manageability: Settling on items and practices that limit natural effect, decrease carbon impressions, and advance maintainable asset use.

Fair Work Works on: Supporting organizations that focus on fair wages, safe working circumstances, and regard for laborers' freedoms all through their stock chains.

Neighborhood and Economical Obtaining: Favoring items that are privately obtained, morally created, and advance supportable agribusiness and assembling.

1.3 Effect of Moral Decisions:

Individual decisions in utilization have broad outcomes that stretch out past private inclinations. The aggregate effect of moral decisions impacts market patterns, prompts organizations to take on dependable practices, and adds to the improvement of an all the more socially and ecologically cognizant economy. Understanding the expanding influences of individual choices highlights the meaning of moral utilization as an impetus for positive change.

Moral Decisions in Food Utilization

2.1 Plant-Based Diets and Creature Government assistance:

Taking on plant-based slims down is a huge moral decision that straightforwardly addresses concerns connected with creature government assistance. Production line cultivating rehearses, which frequently focus on benefit over the prosperity of creatures, have driven numerous people to pick plant-based other options. This part investigates the moral contemplations encompassing meat utilization, the ascent of plant-based counts calories, and the positive effect of picking remorselessness free choices.

2.2 Economical Farming and Natural Effect:

The natural effect of food utilization is a basic thought in moral decisions. Modern agribusiness adds to deforestation, water contamination, and ozone harming substance discharges. Moral purchasers support reasonable agribusiness rehearses, for example, natural cultivating and regenerative farming, which focus on ecological preservation. This part digs into the natural ramifications of food decisions and techniques for decreasing biological impressions through careful utilization.

2.3 Fair Exchange and Civil rights:

Our moral decisions in food utilization reach out past ecological and creature government assistance worries to envelop civil rights issues. Fair exchange rehearses guarantee that ranchers and laborers get fair pay for their work, advancing financial manageability and social value. This part investigates the standards of fair exchange, the effect on cultivating networks, and the job of customers in pushing for civil rights through their food decisions.

Moral Decisions in Item Utilization

3.1 Mercilessness Free and Creature Agreeable Items:

Moral decisions in item utilization incorporate deciding on brutality free options in private consideration, beauty care products, and family things. Buyers progressively look for items that poor person been tried on creatures, supporting organizations that focus on moral practices in item advancement. This part looks at the moral worries related with creature testing, the ascent of mercilessness free confirmations, and the job of purchasers in driving change inside ventures.

3.2 Feasible Design and Dress Decisions:

The design business has confronted investigation for its ecological effect, exploitative work practices, and quick style culture. Moral decisions in apparel utilization include supporting reasonable style brands, picking higher standards without compromise, and advancing practices that focus on fair work and ecological manageability. This segment investigates the moral contemplations in the style business and systems for building a more supportable closet.

3.3 Eco-Accommodating and Maintainable Items:

Past creature government assistance and fair work rehearses, moral decisions in item utilization envelop more extensive contemplations connected with natural manageability. Eco-accommodating items, portrayed by decreased carbon impressions, negligible waste, and the utilization of maintainable materials, mirror a promise to dependable utilization. This segment investigates the standards of eco-accommodating item decisions and the positive effect on both individual ways of life and the planet.

Pragmatic Systems for Moral Utilization

4.1 Exploration and Informed Independent direction:

One of the fundamental parts of moral utilization is very much informed about the items we pick. Investigating organizations, perusing item marks, and remaining informed about industry rehearses engage purchasers to pursue decisions lined up with their qualities. This segment gives commonsense tips to leading exploration and going with informed choices while choosing food and items.

4.2 Supporting Moral Brands and Drives:

Moral utilization includes effectively supporting brands and drives that focus on values like creature government assistance, natural supportability, and fair work rehearses. This segment features the significance of deliberately picking items from organizations focused on moral standards and the positive effect of shopper support in impacting industry rehearses.

4.3 Diminishing Utilization and Embracing Moderation:

A major part of moral utilization is perceiving the natural and social effect of overconsumption. Embracing moderation and lessening pointless buys add to a more economical way of life. This segment investigates the standards of moderation, the advantages of careful utilization, and systems for embracing a more deliberate way to deal with shopping.

4.4 Participating in Backing and Activism:

Past individual decisions, moral shoppers can effectively take part in support and activism to advance foundational change. This segment talks about the job of shopper activism in affecting strategy, supporting moral drives, and pushing for expansive upgrades. Aggregate activity intensifies the effect of moral decisions and adds to a more extensive development for positive change.

Beating Difficulties and Pushing Ahead

5.1 Tending to Moderateness and Openness:

One of the difficulties of moral utilization is the view of greater expenses and restricted openness. This part investigates techniques for beating these difficulties, including the significance of focusing on values, looking for elective choices, and supporting for foundational changes that go with moral decisions more reasonable and open for all.

5.2 Structure a Local area of Moral Purchasers:

Making a local area of similar people who share a promise to moral utilization encourages support, information sharing, and aggregate activity. This part examines the significance of local area commitment, the job of virtual entertainment in associating moral buyers, and the potential for building a development that rises above individual decisions.

5.3 Government Strategies and Guideline:

The job of government strategies and guidelines is urgent in establishing a climate that upholds moral utilization. This segment investigates the potential for strategy changes, for example, naming necessities, impetuses for moral practices, and guidelines that consider organizations responsible for their effect on creatures, the climate, and laborers.

7.2 The impact of veganism and vegetarianism on animal welfare

Veganism and vegetarianism have arisen as strong developments with significant ramifications for creature government assistance. Established in the moral conviction that all conscious creatures merit empathy and regard, these dietary decisions stretch out past private wellbeing to envelop more extensive worries about basic entitlements, natural maintainability, and moral living. In this investigation, we dig into the effect of veganism and vegetarianism on creature government assistance, looking at the moral contemplations, the impact on ventures, and the potential for positive change in encouraging a more caring connection among people and creatures.

Moral Underpinnings of Veganism and Vegetarianism

1.1 Basic entitlements and Sympathy:

At the center of veganism and vegetarianism lies a crucial obligation to basic entitlements and the conviction that all conscious creatures reserve the privilege to live liberated from double-dealing, remorselessness, and superfluous mischief. This moral position mirrors a profound feeling of sympathy for creatures, testing the conventional perspective on creatures as items for human use.

1.2 Decreasing Experiencing in Food Creation:

The domesticated animals industry is a significant wellspring of animal torment, set apart by plant cultivating rehearses that frequently focus on benefit over the prosperity of creatures. Veganism and vegetarianism address a cognizant decision to swear off consuming animal items, consequently lessening the interest for modern cultivating and relieving the intrinsic experiencing related with ordinary creature farming.

1.3 Natural Contemplations:

Past the immediate effect on creature government assistance, embracing a plant-based diet lines up with ecological morals. Domesticated animals farming contributes altogether to deforestation, water contamination, and ozone harming substance discharges. Veganism and vegetarianism, as eco-cognizant decisions, address the natural impression related with animal cultivating, further underlining the interconnectedness of moral decisions.

Diminishing Interest for Creature Items

2.1 Effect on Production line Cultivating Practices:

The interest for animal items drives the escalated cultivating rehearses normal for processing plant cultivating. By picking veganism or vegetarianism, people effectively add to decreasing this interest. This segment investigates how the decrease sought after for meat, dairy, and eggs can provoke changes in cultivating works on, prompting more accommodating and feasible other options.

2.2 Advancing Moral Cultivating Practices:

The shift towards plant-based counts calories signals a dismissal of industrial facility cultivating as well as an underwriting of moral cultivating rehearses. As customers progressively request straightforwardness and moral treatment of animals, ranchers and makers might be boosted to embrace more sympathetic and reasonable techniques. This segment talks about the potential for advancing moral cultivating rehearses through buyer decisions.

2.3 Supporting Other options and Developments:

The ascent of veganism and vegetarianism has prodded the advancement of elective plant-based items and developments in the food business. Plant-based meats, dairy options, and egg substitutes have become progressively well known, furnishing shoppers with moral decisions that line up with their qualities. This segment investigates how the market for plant-based choices has extended, offering more remorselessness free choices.

The Impact of Veganism and Vegetarianism on Businesses

3.1 Financial Effect on Creature Agribusiness:

The developing prominence of veganism and vegetarianism has monetary ramifications for the creature farming industry. As shopper inclinations shift, the financial suitability of regular cultivating rehearses is tested. This segment inspects the financial effect of changing customer ways of behaving on creature farming, inciting ventures to adjust to developing moral contemplations.

3.2 Corporate Responsiveness to Customer Interest:

Expanded buyer mindfulness and interest for morally obtained items have provoked companies to reconsider their practices. This part investigates how corporate elements, from cheap food chains to global food makers, are answering the ascent of veganism and vegetarianism by consolidating plant-based choices, embracing more others conscious norms, and putting resources into supportable practices.

3.3 Interest in Plant-Based Advancements:

The flood in revenue in plant-based counts calories has prompted critical interests in plant-based advancements and new companies. Financial speculators and large companies perceive the capability of a moving business sector, putting resources into creative arrangements that offer options in contrast to customary creature items. This part dives into the effect of these speculations on the turn of events and openness of plant-based choices.

Wellbeing and Social Contemplations of Veganism and Vegetarianism

4.1 Medical advantages and Moral Living:

Veganism and vegetarianism are frequently connected with wellbeing cognizant ways of life. A plant-based diet, when even, can add to diminished dangers of persistent illnesses. This segment investigates the medical advantages related with plant-based abstains from food and the association between private prosperity and moral living.

4.2 Social Developments and Backing:

Veganism and vegetarianism are not simply individual way of life decisions but rather additionally parts of more extensive social developments supporting for basic entitlements and moral living. This part inspects how the reception of plant-based consumes less calories adds to aggregate support, impacting cultural perspectives, strategies, and encouraging a culture of empathy towards creatures.

4.3 Social Moves and Evolving Standards:

As veganism and vegetarianism become more standard, social standards encompassing food decisions are developing. This segment investigates how changing discernments and perspectives towards plant-based eats less add to a social shift that stresses moral contemplations in food utilization and difficulties the conventional perspective on creatures as simple wares.

Difficulties and Reactions

5.1 Wholesome Worries and Dietary Equilibrium:

Pundits of veganism and vegetarianism frequently raise worries about dietary ampleness, stressing the potential for lacks in fundamental supplements like protein, iron, and vitamin B12. This part tends to these worries, giving bits of knowledge into how people can keep a reasonable and healthfully adequate plant-based diet.

5.2 Openness and Moderateness:

One of the difficulties related with veganism and vegetarianism is the impression of restricted availability and greater expenses. This segment examines procedures for beating these difficulties, advancing inclusivity, and supporting for fundamental changes that pursue moral decisions more reasonable and available.

5.3 Social Awareness and Dietary Decisions:

Social standards and customs frequently assume a huge part in forming dietary decisions. This segment investigates the significance of social awareness in advancing veganism and vegetarianism, stressing the requirement for comprehensive methodologies that regard different social practices while empowering moral contemplations.

The Eventual fate of Veganism, Vegetarianism, and Creature Government assistance

6.1 Proceeded with Development of Moral Developments:

The fate of veganism and vegetarianism seems promising, with the two developments expected to develop. This part investigates the elements adding to the supported development of moral developments, including expanding mindfulness, innovative headways, and a more prominent accentuation on supportability.

6.2 Mechanical Advancements and Elective Proteins:

Headways in innovation, especially in the field of elective proteins, assume a significant part in forming the eventual fate of moral utilization. This part inspects how mechanical developments, for example, lab-developed meat and plant-based other options, add to the extension of savagery free choices and further lessen the dependence on conventional creature farming.

6.3 Worldwide Cooperation and Support:

The worldwide idea of moral developments requires cooperative endeavors across borders. This segment investigates the potential for worldwide joint effort, support, and strategy drives that address the more extensive ramifications of veganism and vegetarianism on a worldwide scale, advancing creature government assistance and manageable practices around the world.

7.3 Supporting organizations and businesses that prioritize animal welfare

In the mission for an additional sympathetic and moral world, shoppers assume a vital part by supporting associations and organizations that focus on creature government assistance. As mindfulness develops in regards to the treatment of creatures across different enterprises, people are progressively looking for items and administrations from substances focused on moral practices. This investigation digs into the meaning of supporting such associations, the effect on creature government assistance, and functional procedures for settling on informed decisions that line up with sympathetic qualities.

The Significance of Supporting Creature Well disposed Organizations

1.1 Molding Industry Practices:

Customer decisions use huge impact in molding industry rehearses. By deliberately supporting organizations that focus on creature government assistance, customers send a reasonable message that moral contemplations matter. This segment analyzes the job of buyer inclinations in empowering organizations to embrace more altruistic and manageable works on, cultivating positive change across different businesses.

1.2 Advancing Responsibility:

Supporting creature cordial organizations adds to advancing responsibility inside enterprises. Organizations that focus on creature government assistance are bound to stick to straightforwardness, moral obtaining, and capable assembling rehearses. This segment investigates how customer support boosts organizations to be responsible for their effect on creatures, empowering them to take on better expectations.

1.3 Empowering Moral Development:

Customers are driving a flood popular for moral and maintainable items and administrations. Subsequently, organizations are incited to enhance and foster options that line up with creature agreeable practices. This segment examines how buyer inclinations urge organizations to put resources into innovative work, cultivating a culture of development that benefits the two creatures and the planet.

Recognizing Creature Well disposed Organizations

2.1 Accreditations and Names:

Certificates and names assume a vital part in recognizing organizations that focus on creature government assistance. Different associations give certificates demonstrating adherence to explicit guidelines, for example, savagery free, natural, or fair exchange. This segment investigates ordinarily perceived certificates and names, enabling shoppers to go with informed decisions while supporting organizations.

2.2 Straightforwardness in Supply Chains:

Organizations focused on creature government assistance frequently show straightforwardness in their stockpile chains. Straightforward organizations reveal data about obtaining, producing processes, and moral practices. This segment examines the significance of store network straightforwardness as a key marker while distinguishing and supporting organizations that focus on the prosperity of creatures.

2.3 Corporate Social Obligation (CSR) Drives:

Corporate Social Obligation drives mirror an organization's obligation to moral, social, and ecological obligation. Organizations participated in creature government assistance frequently coordinate CSR drives into their tasks. This part investigates the meaning of CSR programs in distinguishing and supporting organizations that effectively add to positive change.

Techniques for Supporting Creature Amicable Organizations

3.1 Investigating Organization Practices:

A major technique for supporting creature well disposed organizations is directing exhaustive investigation into an organization's practices. This includes exploring obtaining techniques, producing processes, and any affiliations with associations focused on creature government assistance. This part gives functional tips to buyers to explore and assess organizations prior to pursuing buying choices successfully.

3.2 Drawing in with Brands via Online Entertainment:

Online entertainment stages give a strong means to customers to straightforwardly draw in with brands. By effectively partaking in web-based conversations, clarifying some pressing issues, and communicating concerns, shoppers can impact organizations to focus on creature government assistance. This segment investigates how virtual entertainment activism can be a compelling methodology for encouraging positive change inside organizations.

3.3 Democratic with Your Wallet:

Purchaser decisions are likened to projecting votes for moral practices. By purposely picking items and administrations from organizations that focus on creature government assistance, customers apply impact over market patterns. This segment underlines the effect of "casting a ballot with your wallet" and settling on cognizant buying choices as a substantial type of help for creature cordial organizations.

Supporting Creature Government assistance Associations

4.1 Gifts and Gathering pledges:

Direct help for creature government assistance associations through gifts and gathering pledges drives is a strong way for people to add to the reason. This part investigates the effect of monetary help on the activities of associations committed to creature government assistance, empowering them to complete salvage missions, backing, and instructive projects.

4.2 Chipping in and Backing:

Past monetary help, people can effectively participate in chipping in and promotion endeavors for creature government assistance associations. This segment examines the different ways volunteers contribute, from active consideration for creatures to taking part in crusades that bring issues to light about issues influencing creatures.

4.3 Cooperation with Organizations:

Cooperation between creature government assistance associations and organizations can be valuable together. This segment investigates the potential for associations that advance moral practices, for example, organizations giving a level of benefits to creature good cause or effectively taking part in drives that help creature government assistance.

Defeating Difficulties and Reactions

5.1 Greenwashing and Moral Worries:

One test purchasers face is the potential for greenwashing, where organizations dishonestly guarantee to focus on creature government assistance or take on misleading promoting rehearses. This segment gives direction on distinguishing and exploring through greenwashing, guaranteeing that customer support is coordinated towards really moral organizations.

5.2 Moderateness and Openness:

Worries about the moderateness and openness of moral items and administrations are normal obstructions for purchasers. This segment examines methodologies for conquering these difficulties, like looking for spending plan cordial other options, supporting nearby organizations, and pushing for foundational changes that pursue moral decisions more available to a more extensive crowd.

5.3 Adjusting Various Moral Needs:

Purchasers frequently explore complex moral contemplations, like the multifacetedness of ecological, social, and creature government assistance concerns. This part investigates the difficulties of adjusting different moral needs and underlines the significance of pursuing nuanced choices that line up with individual qualities.

The Fate of Creature Cordial Strategic approaches

6.1 Shopper Drove Developments:

The fate of creature amicable strategic approaches is inherently attached to purchaser driven developments. As additional people focus on creature government assistance in their buying choices, organizations will be constrained to answer this change in purchaser values. This part investigates the potential for proceeded with development in customer drove developments that backer for moral strategic approaches.

6.2 Regulation and Guideline:

Administrative guideline and regulation assume a huge part in forming strategic policies. This segment talks about the potential for expanded guidelines that implement moral principles in businesses influencing creature government assistance. More grounded legitimate systems can furnish organizations with clear rules and motivators to focus on moral practices.

6.3 Mechanical Developments:

Progressions in innovation, for example, blockchain and store network straightforwardness apparatuses, hold the possibility to reform how organizations exhibit their obligation to creature government assistance. This segment investigates the job of mechanical advancements in upgrading straightforwardness, decreasing data deviation, and engaging buyers to settle on additional educated decisions.

8

Chapter 8

Education and Advocacy

Instruction and backing structure the bedrock of cultural advancement, encouraging informed personalities and enabling people to advocate for change. Whether tending to social treacheries, ecological worries, or common liberties issues, the mix of training and promotion gives a strong impetus to change. In this complete investigation, we dig into the cooperative connection among schooling and promotion, looking at their jobs, the effect of informed residents, and procedures for developing a general public where information fills positive change.

The Interconnected Elements of Schooling and Promotion

1.1 Characterizing Training and Backing:

Schooling and backing are multi-layered ideas, each assuming an unmistakable yet interconnected part in cultural turn of events. Training includes the obtaining of information, abilities, and values, while backing fixates on effectively supporting a reason or rule. This segment gives a central comprehension of these ideas, laying out the foundation for their cooperative relationship.

1.2 The Job of Schooling in Backing:

Training fills in as the foundation of powerful backing. Informed people are better prepared to grasp complex issues, fundamentally investigate data, and impart influentially. This part investigates how training upgrades the viability of backing by encouraging a profound comprehension of the subtleties encompassing different causes, advancing compassion, and developing a feeling of obligation.

1.3 Promotion's Effect on School Systems:

Alternately, support impacts schooling systems, forming educational programs, and cultivating conditions that empower decisive reasoning and municipal commitment. This part looks at the effect of support on instructive strategies, the consideration of assorted viewpoints, and the advancement of civil rights inside scholarly settings.

The Force of Informed Residents

2.1 Decisive Reasoning and Informed Independent direction:

Instruction engages people with decisive reasoning abilities, empowering them to assess data basically, recognize predispositions, and settle on informed choices. This segment investigates the job of decisive reasoning in backing, underlining the significance of an educated populace in making positive cultural change.

2.2 Media Education and Data Spread:

In the computerized age, media proficiency is a critical part of schooling that impacts promotion endeavors. This segment talks about the effect of media proficiency on data scattering, the difficulties presented by falsehood, and the job of schooling in furnishing people with the abilities to explore the data scene mindfully.

2.3 Community Commitment and Social Obligation:

Schooling imparts a feeling of municipal commitment and social obligation, empowering people to partake in their networks effectively. This segment investigates the connection among schooling and city commitment, stressing how informed residents can drive support developments, add to strategy changes, and impact positive changes.

Instruction as a Device for Civil rights Support

3.1 Tending to Imbalance through Training:

Training fills in as an incredible asset for tending to foundational disparities. This part inspects how schooling can be utilized to destroy oppressive practices, advance inclusivity, and enable underestimated networks, subsequently establishing the groundwork for backing endeavors fixated on civil rights.

3.2 Advancing Variety and Consideration:

Variety and consideration are fundamental parts of both instruction and promotion. This part investigates how instructive establishments can effectively advance variety, cultivate comprehensive conditions, and add to promotion drives that challenge oppressive practices and enhance underrepresented voices.

3.3 Enabling Future Backers:

Instructive foundations assume a significant part in supporting the up and coming age of backers. This part talks about the significance of incorporating backing instruction into educational programs, giving understudies the devices, information, and moral establishments to become viable specialists of positive change.

Backing Drives in Instructive Settings

4.1 Understudy Drove Promotion Developments:

Understudies, as impetuses for change, frequently lead backing developments inside instructive settings. This part investigates the effect of understudy drove drives, from grounds based missions to worldwide developments, and features the job of training in cultivating a feeling of organization among understudies.

4.2 Teachers as Supporters:

Teachers, as forces to be reckoned with and guides, assume a critical part in promotion endeavors. This part analyzes the obligations of teachers in supporting decisive reasoning abilities, advancing sympathy, and filling in as promoters for civil rights inside the instructive structure.

4.3 Local area Commitment and Instructive Promotion:

Instructive foundations are essential pieces of more extensive networks. This part investigates the job of local area commitment in instructive promotion, accentuating the significance of cooperative endeavors between schools, guardians, neighborhood associations, and policymakers to resolve foundational issues.

Procedures for Coordinating Instruction and Promotion

5.1 Integrating Promotion into Educational programs:

To reinforce the connection among schooling and support, this part talks about methodologies for incorporating promotion parts into scholarly educational plans. It investigates interdisciplinary methodologies, contextual analyses, and task based advancing as successful techniques for developing support abilities.

5.2 Using Innovation for Promotion Training:

In the computerized time, innovation fills in as a strong device for support schooling. This segment investigates how advanced stages, online courses, and intelligent advancements can be bridled to improve instructive encounters and outfit people with the abilities required for powerful promotion in the computerized age.

5.3 Structure Associations between Instructive Establishments and Support Associations:

Joint effort between instructive foundations and support associations fortifies the effect of the two elements. This segment examines the potential for associations, accentuating how backing associations can give assets, skill, and certifiable encounters to upgrade instructive drives zeroed in on civil rights and support.

Difficulties and Reactions

6.1 Protection from Change in Schooling Systems:

One test in coordinating schooling and promotion is the protection from change inside laid out school systems. This part investigates the hindrances to change, including institutional idleness, obstruction from partners, and the requirement for fundamental changes to adjust instruction to contemporary backing needs.

6.2 Adjusting Points of view and Keeping away from Predisposition:

Keeping a decent and fair-minded approach in schooling and promotion is urgent. This part tends to the difficulties of introducing different viewpoints, keeping away from inclinations, and guaranteeing that instructive drives and promotion endeavors are comprehensive and fair.

6.3 Guaranteeing Availability to Quality Training:

Openness to quality schooling is a worldwide test that influences support endeavors. This part talks about variations in instructive access, the job of financial elements, and the requirement for backing to address foundational boundaries that ruin evenhanded admittance to training.

The Future Scene of Training and Promotion

7.1 Arising Patterns in Promotion Schooling:

The future scene of promotion schooling is molded by arising patterns. This segment investigates the combination of arising fields like computerized proficiency, natural schooling, and worldwide viewpoints into backing training, getting ready people to address complex difficulties in a quickly impacting world.

7.2 Innovation's Part in Promotion and Schooling:

Headways in innovation keep on rethinking the connection among backing and training. This part talks about the job of arising advancements, including man-made reasoning, augmented simulation, and on-line stages, in upgrading instructive encounters and enhancing support endeavors.

7.3 Worldwide Promotion Organizations and Joint efforts:

As backing rises above geological limits, worldwide organizations and coordinated efforts are turning out to be progressively significant. This segment investigates the potential for worldwide organizations, cooperative promotion drives, and the job of schooling in cultivating a worldwide local area of informed advocates.

8.1 The importance of raising awareness about animal welfare issues

In an interconnected reality where mankind imparts its presence to a different exhibit of animal varieties, bringing issues to light about creature government assistance issues is a pivotal objective. Creatures, whether tamed or wild, are conscious creatures fit for encountering happiness, torment, and a scope of feelings. Upholding for their government assistance goes past moral obligation; it is a crucial obligation to making an amicable concurrence.

This investigation digs into the meaning of bringing issues to light about creature government assistance issues, the effect on creatures and biological systems, and how informed support can drive positive change.

The Inborn Worth of Creatures

1.1 Acknowledgment of Awareness:

Creatures are conscious creatures with the ability to encounter joy, enduring, and a range of feelings. Bringing issues to light about creature government assistance issues starts with perceiving and recognizing the innate worth of creatures, regardless of their species. This segment underscores the significance of understanding and regarding the consciousness of creatures as an establishment for pushing for their sake.

1.2 Environment Interconnectedness:

Creatures assume fundamental parts in environments, adding to biodiversity, biological equilibrium, and the general soundness of the planet. Bringing issues to light about creature government assistance stretches out past individual empathy to include the acknowledgment of the interconnectedness of every living being. This segment investigates how saving creature government assistance adds to keeping up with the fragile equilibrium of biological systems.

1.3 Moral Contemplations:

Advancing creature government assistance lines up with moral contemplations, accentuating the ethical obligation people have toward other living creatures. This part dives into the moral components of how animals are treated in different settings, from modern cultivating to natural life protection, and the basic to address and correct moral difficulties through mindfulness and promotion.

Effect on Creature Government assistance Practices

2.1 Tending to Remorselessness and Double-dealing:

Bringing issues to light is an integral asset for uncovering and tending to savagery and double-dealing towards creatures. Whether in manufacturing plant ranches, bazaars, research centers, or different settings, informed promotion reveals insight into uncaring practices. This part talks about how mindfulness crusades have been instrumental in testing and changing practices that compromise the government assistance of creatures.

2.2 Backing for Authoritative Change:

Informed public mindfulness frequently catalyzes promotion for authoritative change. By enlightening the circumstances creatures persevere and the outcomes of shady practices, the general population can impact policymakers to sanction and fortify regulations that safeguard creature government assistance. This part investigates instances of fruitful authoritative changes driven by open mindfulness crusades.

2.3 Advancing Compassionate Other options:

Bringing issues to light about creature government assistance issues supports the investigation and reception of sympathetic choices in different businesses. From brutality free items to reasonable cultivating rehearses, informed buyers drive interest for additional moral decisions. This part examines how mindfulness prompts ventures to investigate and execute choices that focus on the prosperity of creatures.

Protection and Biodiversity Safeguarding

3.1 Untamed life Preservation Difficulties:

Untamed life faces bunch dangers, including natural surroundings annihilation, poaching, and environmental change. Bringing issues to light about creature government assistance reaches out to untamed life preservation endeavors, revealing insight into the difficulties confronting species all over the planet. This part investigates the job of mindfulness in accumulating support for natural life protection and resolving the perplexing issues undermining biodiversity.

3.2 Effect on Environment Wellbeing:

The government assistance of creatures is unpredictably connected to the soundness of environments. Imperiled species, when driven to the edge, can disturb biological equilibrium. Bringing issues to light about the predicament of these species and the more extensive effects on environments stresses the requirement for protection endeavors. This segment digs into the flowing consequences for environment wellbeing when creature government assistance is compromised.

3.3 Worldwide Obligation regarding Biodiversity:

Worldwide mindfulness crusades assume a crucial part in under-scoring the common obligation of protecting biodiversity. This part examines how bringing issues to light cultivates a feeling of worldwide obligation, empowering cooperation among countries, associations, and people to address the difficulties presented to creature government assistance and biodiversity on a planetary scale.

Moral and Manageable Practices in Agribusiness

4.1 Difficulties in Modern Cultivating:

Modern cultivating rehearses frequently focus on benefit over crea-ture government assistance, prompting conditions that compromise the prosperity of creatures. Bringing issues to light about the moral ramifications of modern cultivating is pivotal in provoking buyers to reevaluate their decisions and supporter for additional altruistic and economical rural practices. This segment investigates the difficulties in-side modern cultivating and the potential for positive change.

4.2 Advancing Plant-Based Diets:

Mindfulness crusades supporting for plant-based eats less add to decreasing the interest for creature items. This part examines how such missions teach the general population about the moral and ecological ramifications of meat utilization, cultivating a shift toward plant-based slims down that line up with standards of creature government assistance.

4.3 Supporting Neighborhood, Reasonable Farming:

Bringing issues to light reaches out to supporting neighborhood and manageable horticulture. By instructing buyers about the advantages of picking privately obtained and morally created food, mindfulness crusades add to the advancement of cultivating rehearses that focus on creature government assistance. This segment investigates the effect of such drives on reshaping rural scenes.

Public Commitment and Grassroots Support

5.1 Engaging People:

Bringing issues to light about creature government assistance engages people to settle on decisions lined up with their qualities. Whether through informed purchaser choices, way of life changes, or support in backing drives, people assume a pivotal part in driving change. This segment investigates how mindfulness crusades enable individuals to become advocates for creatures in their day to day routines.

5.2 Local area Drove Drives:

Networks can be center points of progress with regards to creature government assistance. This segment examines the significance of local area drove drives, from nearby salvage gatherings to instructive projects, in making an aggregate effect on how creatures are treated inside unambiguous districts. Grassroots endeavors intensify the compass and viability of mindfulness crusades.

5.3 Web-based Entertainment and Advanced Support:

In the advanced age, web-based entertainment stages act as amazing assets for bringing issues to light about creature government assistance. This segment investigates the effect of computerized promotion crusades, viral substance, and online networks in contacting a worldwide crowd and encouraging a shared perspective about creature government assistance issues.

Difficulties and Procedures for Conquering Them

6.1 Sympathy Weakness and Desensitization:

One test in bringing issues to light about creature government assistance is the gamble of sympathy weakness and desensitization. Consistent openness to upsetting pictures and data can numb people to the direness of the issues. This segment talks about procedures for tending to empathy exhaustion and keeping up with supported commitment in creature government assistance backing.

6.2 Adjusting Social Awareness:

Social standards and customs frequently impact the treatment of creatures. Bringing issues to light should be drawn nearer with social awareness, perceiving assorted viewpoints while pushing for moral treatment. This segment investigates methodologies for finding some kind of harmony between social awareness and the advancement of all inclusive moral norms for creature government assistance.

6.3 Defeating Suspicion and Obstruction:

Protection from change, doubt, and industry resistance can present huge difficulties to creature government assistance promotion. This segment examines procedures for conquering obstruction, including proof based correspondence, joint effort with partners, and utilizing public help to impact fundamental change.

The Eventual fate of Creature Government assistance Backing

7.1 Mix into Formal Training:

The fate of creature government assistance backing lies in its mix into formal training. By consolidating curricular parts that stress sympathy, moral obligation, and the interconnectedness of every living being, instructive establishments add to molding an age of supporters. This segment investigates the potential for formal schooling to be an impetus for supported creature government assistance promotion.

7.2 Mechanical Progressions in Backing:

Progressions in innovation, from computer generated reality encounters to information driven crusades, hold monstrous potential for improving the adequacy of creature government assistance promotion.

This part talks about how mechanical advancements can be utilized to make vivid encounters, collect more extensive help, and drive unmistakable change.

7.3 Worldwide Cooperation for Fundamental Change:

The eventual fate of creature government assistance backing requires worldwide cooperation and foundational change. This segment investigates the potential for worldwide collusions, strategy systems, and cross-area coordinated efforts to address the underlying drivers of creature government assistance issues and lay out moral principles on a worldwide scale.

8.2 Strategies for effective animal advocacy and activism

Creature support and activism are fundamental parts of a humane society, endeavoring to guarantee the prosperity and moral treatment of creatures. Compelling support requires a mix of informed procedures, public commitment, and a promise to foundational change. In this investigation, we dive into key systems that enable people and associations to be significant promoters for creatures, tending to a scope of issues from brutality in different businesses to untamed life protection.

Figuring out the Issues and Laying out Objectives

1.1 Inside and out Exploration and Instruction:

Compelling creature support begins with an intensive comprehension of the main things in need of attention. Inside and out examination into different parts of animal government assistance, including modern cultivating rehearses, natural life preservation difficulties, and issues connected with friend creatures, shapes the establishment for informed support. This segment examines the significance of training and constant figuring out how to remain refreshed on developing issues.

1.2 Defining Clear Promotion Objectives:

Characterize clear and feasible support objectives in light of the particular issues you mean to address. Whether it's upholding for official changes, advancing plant-based diets, or battling against natural life double-dealing, laying out unambiguous and quantifiable objectives gives a guide to significant promotion. This segment investigates the most common way of laying out objectives that line up with the mission of creature promotion endeavors.

1.3 Zeroing in on Fundamental Change:

While tending to prompt worries is pivotal, viable promotion looks past superficial issues to target fundamental change. This part examines the significance of distinguishing and focusing on main drivers, drawing in with policymakers, and pushing for primary changes that lastingly affect creature government assistance.

Drawing in with Assorted Crowds
2.1 Fitting Directives for Various Crowds:
Creature advocates need to tailor their messages to reverberate with assorted crowds. Whether tending to policymakers, the overall population, or explicit networks, making messages that allure for the qualities and worries of every crowd fragment upgrades the adequacy of support endeavors. This part investigates the significance of nuanced correspondence for more extensive effort.

2.2 Using Web-based Entertainment and Computerized Stages:
In the advanced age, virtual entertainment and online stages are amazing assets for creature promotion. This part examines procedures for utilizing web-based entertainment to bring issues to light, share convincing stories, and draw in a worldwide crowd. Compelling utilization of computerized stages works with ongoing correspondence, grassroots getting sorted out, and the intensification of promotion messages.

2.3 Teaming up with Powerhouses and Big names:
Teaming up with powerhouses and big names who share an energy for creature government assistance can fundamentally enhance promotion endeavors. This segment investigates the advantages of vital associations, the span of big name supports, and how force to be reckoned with joint efforts can focus on basic creature government assistance issues.

Grassroots Activism and Local area Commitment
3.1 Engaging Nearby People group:
Grassroots activism includes engaging nearby networks to be advocates for creatures. This part examines the effect of local area drove drives, nearby occasions, and instructive projects in encouraging a feeling of aggregate liability and making change from the beginning.

3.2 Local area Studios and Instructive Projects:
Training is a strong device for backing. Putting together local area studios, workshops, and instructive projects disperses data, dissipate fantasies, and construct an underpinning of information that cultivates sympathy and understanding. This segment investigates the effect of active commitment and instructive drives in neighborhood networks.

3.3 Supporting Creature Protects and Safe houses: Straightforwardly supporting neighborhood creature safeguards and sanctuaries is a substantial method for adding to backing endeavors. This part examines the significance of local area association in cultivating reception, fixing/fixing programs, and giving assets to associations on the bleeding edge of creature government assistance.

Official Backing and Strategy Change

4.1 Drawing in with Policymakers:

Viable creature backing frequently includes drawing in with policymakers to impact administrative change. This segment investigates procedures for building associations with legislators, introducing proof based contentions, and upholding for the execution of regulations that safeguard creature government assistance.

4.2 Supporting and Starting Regulation:

Promotion gatherings can effectively support or start regulation that lines up with their objectives. This part examines the most common way of creating and supporting bills that address explicit creature government assistance issues, working cooperatively with lawmakers to establish significant change.

4.3 Checking and Answering Regulative Turns of events:

Creature advocates should remain watchful in checking administrative turns of events and answering speedily to arising issues. This segment investigates the significance of remaining informed about proposed regulation, preparing allies, and effectively taking part in the vote based cycle to guarantee that creature government assistance stays a need.

Corporate Backing and Buyer Impact

5.1 Drawing in with Companies:

Companies assume a critical part in creature government assistance, particularly in ventures like food creation, style, and diversion. Creature backers can draw in with organizations through discourse, exchange, and, if important, public strain to support moral practices. This segment investigates successful procedures for corporate support.

5.2 Blacklists and Purchaser Impact:

Purchaser decisions have the ability to shape ventures. Backing endeavors can use purchaser impact through designated blacklists, supporting moral brands, and provoking interest for mercilessness free items. This segment examines the effect of customer decisions on corporate practices and how promoters can saddle this impact for positive change.

5.3 Corporate Associations for Positive Change:

At times, teaming up with partnerships can prompt positive change. This segment investigates the potential for framing organizations with organizations ready to embrace moral and feasible works on, underlining the significance of cooperation in driving far reaching enhancements.

Global Coordinated effort and Promotion

6.1 Joining Worldwide Organizations:

Creature support is a worldwide undertaking, and global cooperation fortifies promotion endeavors. This segment examines the advantages of joining worldwide organizations, sharing assets, and planning efforts to address worldwide creature government assistance challenges.

6.2 Partaking in Worldwide Missions:

Promoters can enhance their effect by partaking in worldwide missions that address transnational issues, for example, natural life dealing, environmental change, and the abuse of creatures in different enterprises. This segment investigates how global coordinated effort upgrades the adequacy of backing efforts.

6.3 Drawing in with Global Associations:

Teaming up with laid out global associations committed to creature government assistance gives advocates assets, skill, and a stage for more extensive effect. This segment talks about procedures for drawing in with associations like the World Creature Security, Accommodating Society Global, and others to add to worldwide promotion endeavors.

Beating Difficulties and Guaranteeing Maintainability

7.1 Tending to Promotion Burnout:

Promotion work can be genuinely burdening, prompting burnout. This part investigates systems for tending to and forestalling burnout, underlining the significance of taking care of oneself, keeping a steady local area, and pacing backing endeavors for long haul manageability.

7.2 Exploring Lawful and Moral Difficulties:

Lawful and moral difficulties can present snags to promotion endeavors. This part examines procedures for exploring lawful intricacies, tending to expected moral situations, and guaranteeing that support crusades comply to laid out standards.

7.3 Guaranteeing Inclusivity and Diversity:

Powerful support requires inclusivity and a comprehension of multifacetedness. This segment investigates methodologies for guaranteeing that backing endeavors are comprehensive, taking into account the assorted points of view and needs of networks, and perceiving the interconnectedness of different civil rights issues.

8.3 The role of education in fostering empathy and responsible animal care

Training assumes a crucial part in molding people's viewpoints, perspectives, and ways of behaving towards creatures. Past the obtaining of information, schooling fills in as an impetus for encouraging sympathy and imparting a feeling of obligation for the government assistance of our kindred animals. In this investigation, we dig into the extraordinary force of training in developing compassion and advancing capable creature care, looking at the effect on people, networks, and society in general.

The Groundworks of Sympathy Through Instruction

1.1 Figuring out Creature Awareness:

Instruction gives the establishment to understanding that creatures are conscious creatures, equipped for encountering a scope of feelings. This information frames the foundation of sympathy, as people figure out how to perceive and regard the sentiments, needs, and intrinsic worth of creatures. This part underlines the significance of integrating examples on creature awareness into instructive educational programs.

1.2 Experiential Learning Open doors:

Past conventional study hall settings, experiential learning open doors improve sympathy by permitting people to associate straightforwardly with creatures. Field outings to creature safe-havens, nature holds, and involved exercises work with a more profound association with creatures. This segment investigates the effect of experiential learning in cultivating sympathy and empowering capable creature care rehearses.

1.3 Advancing a Culture of Sympathy:

Training adds to the improvement of a culture of sympathy by imparting upsides of thoughtfulness, compassion, and regard for every living being. This social shift is fundamental for building a general public where capable creature care isn't simply an obligation however a common moral responsibility. This part looks at how instructive organizations can effectively advance a culture of empathy.

Integrating Creature Government assistance into Educational programs

2.1 Incorporating Creature Morals into Formal Schooling:

A vital part of cultivating sympathy is the reconciliation of creature morals into formal schooling educational plans. Subjects like science, natural science, and morals give amazing chances to investigate the moral contemplations encompassing creature treatment. This part examines the advantages and difficulties of integrating creature government assistance training into different scholarly disciplines.

2.2 Drawing in Interdisciplinary Methodologies:

Training can take on interdisciplinary ways to deal with advance the comprehension of mindful creature care. Consolidating components of science, morals, social science, and ecological examinations offers a comprehensive perspective on the interconnectedness between human activities and creature government assistance. This segment investigates the benefits of interdisciplinary schooling in advancing compassion and dependable practices.

2.3 Instructive Drives Past Study halls:

Thorough instructive drives reach out past proper homeroom settings. Studios, workshops, and extracurricular projects zeroed in on creature government assistance add to balanced schooling. This part examines the significance of different instructive methodologies in contacting an expansive crowd and sustaining an age focused on capable creature care.

Building Compassion Through Creature Helped Training

3.1 Restorative and Instructive Jobs of Creatures:

Creatures can serve restorative and instructive jobs in different settings. From treatment creatures in medical services to instructive projects consolidating creatures in schools, these collaborations encourage sympathy and profound association. This part investigates the advantages of creature helped training in sustaining sympathy and capable perspectives.

3.2 Creature Helped Treatment Projects:

Integrating creatures into helpful intercessions gives exceptional open doors to people to foster sympathy and empathy. Creature helped treatment programs, frequently utilized in medical care and instructive settings, have shown positive results in working on close to home prosperity and interactive abilities. This part digs into the effect of such projects on cultivating sympathy.

3.3 Instructive Drives with Creature Representatives:

Bringing creatures into instructive settings as representatives for their species is a strong method for drawing in understudies inwardly. These creature envoys can be important for instructive effort programs, visiting schools to make direct associations among understudies and creatures. This part investigates how creature diplomats add to building sympathy and capable consideration.

Showing Mindful Creature Care Practices

4.1 Grasping Essential Creature Needs:

Training furnishes people with the information on essential creature needs, including sustenance, asylum, and clinical consideration. By understanding the basic necessities for creature prosperity, people are more ready to get a sense of ownership with the creatures in their consideration. This part accentuates the job of schooling in bestowing useful information on mindful consideration rehearses.

4.2 Empowering Mindful Pet Possession:

Mindful pet possession is a critical part of creature care, and training assumes a urgent part in advancing it. Showing imminent pet people the responsibility, assets, and moral contemplations associated with pet consideration adds to the prosperity of friend creatures. This segment talks about the instructive drives pointed toward encouraging capable pet proprietorship.

4.3 Upholding for Moral Treatment of Livestock:

Training can drive mindfulness about the moral treatment of creatures in agrarian settings. Understanding the states of manufacturing plant cultivating and the effect of dietary decisions on creature government assistance engages people to go with informed choices. This part investigates how instruction can move dependable decisions in regards to the treatment of livestock.

Difficulties and Arrangements in Creature Government assistance Training

5.1 Beating Social and Generational Perspectives:

Challenges in advancing dependable creature care through schooling incorporate social and generational mentalities. This segment talks about procedures for defeating protection from change, cultivating open exchange, and tending to social standards that might hinder the reception of dependable practices.

5.2 Tending to Instructive Holes:

Not all school systems focus on creature government assistance, prompting holes in information and mindfulness. This part investigates the requirement for tending to instructive abberations, supporting for normalized educational plan parts, and guaranteeing that all understudies approach exhaustive training on mindful creature care.

5.3 Adjusting Moral Contemplations:

In showing dependable creature care, teachers should adjust moral contemplations and try not to force explicit qualities. This segment examines the significance of introducing different viewpoints, empowering decisive reasoning, and encouraging a nuanced comprehension of the moral intricacies encompassing creature care.

Local area Contribution and Effort Projects

6.1 Connecting with the Local area:

Training stretches out past proper establishments to the more extensive local area. Outreach programs that draw in local area individuals, including grown-ups and kids, add to building an aggregate comprehension of mindful creature care. This segment investigates the effect of local area contribution in encouraging compassion and capable practices.

6.2 Working together with Creature Government assistance Associations:

Associations with creature government assistance associations intensify the effect of instructive drives. Cooperative endeavors between instructive establishments and these associations work with outreach, mindfulness crusades, and commonsense drives for dependable creature care. This part examines the cooperative energies among training and backing associations.

6.3 Making Supportable People group Tasks:

Supportable people group projects zeroed in on creature government assistance give active encounters that build up capable consideration rehearses. From people group nurseries to natural life preservation drives, these undertakings cultivate a feeling of aggregate liability. This part investigates the job of reasonable local area projects in advancing capable creature care.

9

Chapter9

Challenges and Controversies

Creature government assistance and backing, in spite of their respectable objectives, work in a complex and frequently questionable scene. This investigation digs into the complex difficulties and debates that go up against people, associations, and social orders focused on the prosperity of creatures. From moral difficulties and social contrasts to official deficiencies and industry opposition, understanding and resolving these issues is fundamental for cultivating viable change and molding a more merciful world.

Moral Quandaries in Creature Government assistance Promotion

1.1 Adjusting Preservation and Basic entitlements:

One of the conspicuous moral quandaries in creature government assistance promotion spins around the harmony between protection endeavors and individual basic entitlements. While preservation plans to save species and biological systems, it now and again includes rehearses that might think twice about prosperity of individual creatures. This part investigates the moral contemplations and difficulties of tracking down an agreeable harmony among preservation and basic entitlements.

1.2 Willful extermination and Populace Control:

The issue of willful extermination and populace control represents a critical moral test in creature government assistance. In instances of overpopulation, particularly in covers, willful extermination is here and there viewed as for the purpose of populace control. This segment examines the moral ramifications, discussions encompassing willful extermination choices, and investigates elective ways to deal with overseeing creature populaces.

1.3 Hereditary Alteration and Creature Government assistance:

Progressions in hereditary designing bring up moral issues concerning creature government assistance. This segment digs into the discussions encompassing hereditary change, including the moral contemplations of making hereditarily altered creatures for different purposes, from agrarian practices to logical examination.

Social Contrasts and Viewpoints

2.1 Social Differences in Creature Treatment:

Social contrasts essentially impact perspectives and practices connected with creature government assistance. What may be viewed as satisfactory treatment in one culture could be seen as mercilessness in another. This part investigates the difficulties of exploring social changes, the job of social responsiveness, and methodologies for cultivating a worldwide comprehension of creature government assistance.

2.2 Strict Convictions and Creature Use:

Strict convictions can affect how creatures are dealt with and utilized in different social orders. From ceremonial penances to dietary practices, this part looks at the convergence of strict convictions and creature government assistance, featuring the difficulties in accommodating different points of view while upholding for moral treatment.

2.3 Customary Practices and Preservation:

Certain customary practices, well established in social legacy, can conflict with current protection endeavors. Adjusting regard for social customs with the basic to safeguard imperiled species presents difficulties. This part investigates the intricacies of exploring customary practices with regards to preservation and creature government assistance.

Authoritative and Administrative Difficulties

3.1 Deficiencies in Creature Government assistance Regulation:

In spite of developing mindfulness, numerous locales actually wrestle with deficiencies in creature government assistance regulation. This segment investigates the difficulties presented by feeble or non-existent legitimate structures, the irregularities in requirement, and the requirement for complete and strong creature government assistance regulations.

3.2 Campaigning and Industry Impact:

The impact of enterprises participated in rehearses that might think twice about government assistance represents a critical test to regulative drives. This segment inspects how campaigning endeavors by strong enterprises can thwart the entry of viable creature government assistance regulation, featuring the requirement for straightforwardness and responsibility.

3.3 Worldwide Variations in Legitimate Guidelines:

Worldwide variations in creature government assistance norms add to difficulties in making a strong and generally acknowledged system. This segment investigates the intricacies of adjusting assorted legitimate guidelines, the effect of worldwide exchange on creature government assistance, and the requirement for global joint effort to address these incongruities.

Creature Farming and Modern Practices

4.1 Production line Cultivating and Concentrated Control:

Production line cultivating and concentrated control rehearses stay petulant issues in creature government assistance. This segment investigates the difficulties of upholding for change in an industry that frequently focuses on benefit over the prosperity of creatures, resolving issues, for example, packing, lacking everyday environments, and the utilization of development advancing substances.

4.2 Slaughterhouse Conditions and Compassionate Practices:

The circumstances inside slaughterhouses raise moral worries about the treatment of creatures bound for human utilization. This segment examines the difficulties in supporting for altruistic practices, the effect of industrialized butcher cycles, and the requirement for straightforwardness in the meat creation industry.

4.3 Creature Testing and Logical Exploration:

The utilization of creatures in logical examination, while adding to progressions in medication, brings up moral issues. Finding some kind of harmony between logical advancement and moral treatment presents difficulties in upholding for options and pushing for additional compassionate practices in the domain of creature testing. This segment investigates the contentions encompassing creature testing and the continuous endeavors to advance other options.

Natural life Protection Difficulties

5.1 Pressures Among Preservation and Native Freedoms:

Preservation endeavors frequently meet with native regions, prompting strains between natural life protection objectives and the freedoms of native networks. This segment investigates the difficulties of exploring these pressures, regarding native information, and cultivating joint effort for economical protection rehearses.

5.2 Poaching and Unlawful Natural life Exchange:

Poaching and the unlawful natural life exchange present imposing difficulties to untamed life protection. This segment digs into the intricacies of resolving these issues, the job of worldwide cooperation, and the moral contemplations encompassing measures taken to battle poaching and natural life dealing.

5.3 Hostage Rearing and Renewed introduction:

Hostage rearing and renewed introduction programs are fundamental to natural life protection, yet they are not without contention. This segment looks at the difficulties of adjusting the advantages of hostage rearing with worries about creature government assistance, hereditary variety, and the possible effects on once again introduced populaces.

Public Discernment and Media Impact

6.1 Humanoid attribution and Misinformed Empathy:

Humanoid attribution, ascribing human qualities to creatures, can prompt good natured however misinformed sympathy. This segment investigates the difficulties of overseeing public insights impacted by humanoid attribution and the need to figure out some kind of harmony among sympathy and practical comprehension.

6.2 Media Melodrama and Promotion Effect:

Media assumes a significant part in forming popular assessment on creature government assistance issues. Nonetheless, drama can misshape realities and effect promotion endeavors adversely. This segment talks about the difficulties of media portrayal, the job of emotionalism, and methodologies for keeping up with exact depictions in the media.

6.3 Backfire and Analysis in Creature Support:

Creature government assistance advocates frequently face kickback and analysis, in some cases from startling quarters. This part investigates the difficulties of exploring analysis, tending to misguided judgments, and keeping up with validity notwithstanding different conclusions inside general society and, surprisingly, inside the creature support local area.

Adjusting Human Requirements and Creature Government assistance

7.1 Monetary Tensions and Creature Double-dealing:

Monetary tensions can drive rehearses that exploit creatures for benefit, like in the travel industry, amusement, and farming. This part analyzes the difficulties of offsetting monetary necessities with moral contemplations, the effect of shopper interest, and procedures for advancing feasible practices.

7.2 Creature Use in Diversion:

The utilization of creatures in amusement, from bazaars to amusement parks, raises moral worries about their treatment and prosperity. This part investigates the difficulties of supporting for the getting rid of shady practices while thinking about the financial interests of media outlets.

7.3 Human-Creature Struggle in Preservation:

Preservation endeavors can prompt contentions among people and creatures, particularly in regions where natural life environments cross with human settlements. This part talks about the difficulties of relieving human-creature struggle, adjusting the requirements of nearby networks with protection objectives, and cultivating conjunction.

Advances in Innovation and Moral Ramifications

8.1 Arising Advances in Creature Exploration:

Progressions in innovation, including hereditary designing and manmade reasoning, have moral ramifications for creature government assistance. This segment investigates the difficulties and discussions encompassing the utilization of arising advancements in creature research, underscoring the requirement for moral rules and mindful development.

8.2 Observation and Security Concerns:

The utilization of observation advancements in checking creature government assistance, particularly in modern settings, raises security concerns. This segment examines the difficulties of adjusting the requirement for straightforwardness with deference for security privileges, guaranteeing that reconnaissance measures add to further developed government assistance without compromising individual opportunities.

8.3 Bioethics and Cloning:

The field of bioethics stands up to moral contemplations connected with cloning and hereditary control for the protection of imperiled species. This part investigates the difficulties and contentions encompassing these works on, stressing the requirement for mindful and morally directed approaches.

9.1 Ethical dilemmas in wildlife management and population control

Natural life the executives and populace control are fundamental parts of protection endeavors pointed toward keeping up with environmental equilibrium and safeguarding biodiversity. Notwithstanding, these practices frequently bring about complex moral problems that require cautious thought. Finding some kind of harmony between preservation objectives and moral treatment of individual creatures is a test that natural life directors and moderates face. In this investigation, we dive into the moral predicaments inborn in natural life the board and populace control, looking at the subtleties, contentions, and likely answers for explore this mind boggling territory.

The Requirement for Untamed life The executives and Populace Control

1.1 Protection Goals:

Untamed life the board and populace control are driven by the need to address biological uneven characters brought about by human exercises, territory misfortune, and environmental change. Preservation endeavors intend to safeguard jeopardized species, save biodiversity, and guarantee the general wellbeing of biological systems. This part underlines the basic job of populace control in accomplishing these preservation goals.

1.2 Human-Natural life Struggle Moderation:

As human populaces extend and infringe upon normal environments, clashes among people and natural life become more pervasive. Populace control measures are frequently executed to relieve these contentions, diminishing cases of property harm, dangers to human security, and retaliatory killings of untamed life. This segment investigates the moral contemplations in tending to human-untamed life clashes through populace control.

1.3 Sickness Anticipation in Natural life:

Populace control measures are additionally utilized to forestall the spread of sicknesses inside natural life populaces. This is significant for keeping up with the wellbeing and versatility of biological systems. Moral problems emerge while tending to sickness episodes, as choices made to ultimately benefit the populace might include hard decisions that influence individual creatures. This segment dives into the moral contemplations in illness counteraction techniques.

Moral Problems in Untamed life Populace Control

2.1 Winnowing and Specific Killing:

Winnowing, or the particular killing of explicit people inside a populace, is a typical populace control technique. This approach raises moral worries connected with the ethical remaining of individual creatures and the potential for social interruption inside natural life networks. This segment investigates the quandaries encompassing winnowing and the moral contemplations in choosing which creatures to target.

2.2 Contraception and Conceptive Control:

Contraception techniques are progressively investigated as options in contrast to deadly populace control measures. Nonetheless, moral problems continue to happen in the utilization of conceptive control, incorporating worries about obstructing normal ways of behaving, unseen side-effects, and the drawn out influences on individual creatures and populaces. This segment examines the moral contemplations in executing prophylactic estimates in untamed life.

2.3 Movement and Living space The board:

Movement, or the development of creatures to new natural surroundings, is one more procedure utilized in populace control. While this technique plans to keep away from deadly measures, it raises moral predicaments connected with pressure, relocation, and the potential for acquainting new difficulties with moved populaces. This segment analyzes the moral contemplations in movement endeavors and environment the board.

Moral Contemplations in Unambiguous Natural life The executives Situations

3.1 Deer The board and Overpopulation:

In districts where deer populaces have flooded because of territory changes and absence of regular hunters, moral situations arise in overseeing overpopulation. This part investigates the difficulties of adjusting the biological effect of deer overpopulation with the moral treatment of these creatures, taking into account choices, for example, separating, contraception, and living space the executives.

3.2 Elephant The board and Preservation:

In regions where human-elephant clashes are predominant, moral issues emerge in overseeing elephant populaces. Choices connected with winnowing, movement, or contraception should consider the intricate social designs of elephant crowds and the moral treatment of profoundly savvy and social creatures. This segment examines the moral contemplations in elephant populace control.

3.3 Flesh eater Protection and Hunter Control:

Offsetting flesh eater preservation with the insurance of animals and human security presents moral difficulties. Hunter control measures, for example, deadly evacuation of people, mean to address clashes yet raise worries about the effect on hunter populaces and environments. This part looks at the moral issues in meat eater protection and populace control.

Partner Commitment and Moral Independent direction

4.1 Including Nearby People group:

Moral natural life the board requires significant commitment with nearby networks, perceiving their viewpoints, information, and freedoms. Offsetting protection objectives with the requirements and upsides of neighborhood populaces is pivotal for building moral and supportable administration rehearses. This segment investigates the significance of local area contribution in dynamic cycles.

4.2 Assent and Straightforwardness:

Moral natural life the executives requests straightforwardness in dynamic cycles and acquiring informed assent from partners, including nearby networks, preservation associations, and legislative bodies. Open correspondence about the objectives, techniques, and expected effects of populace control measures is fundamental for moral practice. This segment examines the meaning of assent and straightforwardness in natural life the board.

4.3 Cooperation with Native Information:

Native information and customary biological practices frequently hold significant experiences for moral untamed life the board. Teaming up with native networks cultivates a more all encompassing comprehension of environments and adds to moral independent direction. This segment investigates the moral contemplations in coordinating native information into untamed life the executives procedures.

The Job of Science and Exploration Morals

5.1 Exploration Strategies and Creature Government assistance:

Logical exploration assumes a fundamental part in illuminating untamed life the executives choices. Notwithstanding, the techniques utilized in exploration can raise moral worries, especially when they include obtrusive methods or mediations that influence creature government assistance. This segment looks at the moral contemplations in research strategies and the obligation of researchers to focus on creature government assistance.

5.2 Long haul Checking and Versatile Administration:

Moral natural life the board requires a guarantee to long haul checking and versatile administration rehearses. This includes consistently rethinking the effect of populace control measures, changing systems in view of new data, and focusing on the prosperity of natural life populaces. This part investigates the moral contemplations in keeping up with versatile administration draws near.

5.3 Alleviating Potentially negative results:

Populace control measures might have potentially negative results, for example, upsetting social designs, changing biological system elements, or affecting non-target species. Moral direction includes a promise to moderating these potentially negative side-effects and adjusting methodologies to limit hurt. This segment talks about the moral contemplations in tending to and forestalling potentially negative results.

Public Insight and Instruction

6.1 Public Mindfulness and Moral Natural life The executives:

Public discernment assumes a huge part in molding moral norms for untamed life the board. Instructing people in general about the intricacies of populace control, the significance of protection, and the moral contemplations included encourages understanding and backing. This segment investigates the job of public mindfulness in moral untamed life the board.

6.2 Schooling and Support Drives:

Moral untamed life the board is fortified by instruction and backing drives that advance mindfulness, draw in people in general, and encourage a feeling of obligation. This part talks about the significance of instructive projects and support endeavors in molding public mentalities and empowering moral practices in untamed life the executives.

6.3 Media Portrayal and Moral Problems:

Media portrayal of natural life the executives practices can impact public discernment and add to moral quandaries. Capable detailing, precise depiction of the executives endeavors, and staying away from sentimentality are essential for keeping up with public trust and backing. This segment looks at the job of media in forming moral problems and the obligations of news sources in covering natural life the executives.

9.2 The intersection of cultural practices and animal welfare

The crossing point of social practices and creature government assistance is a complex and nuanced landscape where customs, convictions, and moral contemplations combine. Social practices frequently shape the connection among people and creatures, impacting how creatures are dealt with, utilized, and respected inside a given society. This investigation dives into the complex elements of the convergence between social practices and creature government assistance, inspecting the moral difficulties, clashes, and likely roads for encouraging comprehension and positive change.

The Social Meaning of Creatures

1.1 Creatures in Imagery and Folklore:

Many societies saturate creatures with emblematic significance and integrate them into fantasies and old stories. Creatures frequently address social qualities, ethics, or act as emblems. This part investigates the social meaning of creatures in different social orders, underscoring the well established associations between social personality and the treatment of creatures.

1.2 Strict Convictions and Creature Use:

Strict convictions can significantly impact the treatment of creatures inside a culture. A few religions endorse explicit works on including creatures, like penances, dietary limitations, or the utilization of creatures in customs. This segment inspects the crossing point of strict convictions and creature government assistance, recognizing the moral predicaments that emerge when strict practices influence the prosperity of creatures.

1.3 Customary Practices and Social Legacy:

Social legacy frequently includes customary practices connected with creatures, including hunting, grouping, or stately occasions. These practices are gone down through ages and add to the character of a local area. This part investigates the difficulties of tending to customary practices that might struggle with contemporary understandings of creature government assistance.

Moral Issues in Social Practices

2.1 Creature Penances and Customs:

Creature penances are basic to the strict and social acts of different networks. While these customs hold profound social importance, they raise moral worries with respect to the accommodating treatment of creatures. This segment investigates the moral quandaries encompassing creature penances and the need to track down a harmony between social regard and creature government assistance.

2.2 Conventional Hunting and Resource Practices:

In certain societies, hunting and assembling are fundamental for means and social endurance. Be that as it may, present day worries about biodiversity misfortune and creature government assistance bring up moral issues about the effect of conventional hunting rehearses. This segment examines the difficulties of accommodating the requirement for social safeguarding with the basic to safeguard natural life.

2.3 Natural life Exchange and Customary Medication:

The utilization of creature parts in conventional medication is profoundly imbued in specific social practices. Be that as it may, the interest for untamed life items can add to unlawful untamed life exchange, presenting dangers to biodiversity and creature government assistance. This part investigates the moral situations related with the convergence of customary medication and natural life preservation.

Social Responsiveness and Moral Commitment

3.1 Regarding Social Variety:

Moving toward the crossing point of social practices and creature government assistance requires a nuanced comprehension of social variety. Regarding different perspectives and perceiving the worth of social legacy is fundamental for cultivating exchange and building spans between creature government assistance supporters and networks with well established customs. This part underscores the significance of social responsiveness in tending to moral difficulties.

3.2 Cooperative Preservation Endeavors:

Viable commitment includes joint effort between creature government assistance supporters and networks to foster maintainable arrangements. This coordinated effort might incorporate incorporating social viewpoints into preservation techniques, advancing local area based drives, and settling on some mutual interest that regards both social practices and moral treatment of creatures. This part investigates instances of fruitful cooperative protection endeavors.

3.3 Instructive Drives for Social Getting it:

Schooling assumes a urgent part in advancing social comprehension and moral mindfulness. Carrying out instructive drives that feature the interconnectedness of social practices, creature government assistance, and more extensive natural frameworks can cultivate sympathy and energize positive changes. This part talks about the likely effect of instructive projects in connecting social holes.

Legitimate Structures and Social Awareness

4.1 Legitimate Difficulties and Social Practices:

Laying out legitimate systems that address the moral treatment of creatures while regarding social practices is a complicated errand. Clashes might emerge when legitimate guidelines conflict with profoundly imbued customs. This segment investigates the difficulties in exploring legitimate structures that oblige social variety while advancing creature government assistance.

4.2 Arranging Moral Guidelines:

Arranging moral guidelines that work out some kind of harmony between social practices and creature government assistance requires open exchange and shared regard. This part inspects the significance of making spaces for valuable discussions where various viewpoints can be heard and moral norms can be cooperatively settled.

4.3 Worldwide Joint effort for Moral Agreement:

Given the worldwide idea of numerous creature government assistance issues, global coordinated effort is imperative for tending to moral quandaries coming from social practices. This includes making a stage for countries and networks to share encounters, arrange moral norms, and work towards an agreement that regards social variety while maintaining creature government assistance. This segment investigates the potential for global coordinated effort in laying out moral standards.

Social Development and Transformation

5.1 Social Development and Change:

Societies are dynamic substances that develop after some time. This segment investigates the potential for social advancement and variation, where networks reexamine specific practices considering evolving values, environmental mindfulness, and moral contemplations. Inspecting situations where societies have adjusted to present day challenges while protecting fundamental practices offers bits of knowledge into the chance of positive change.

5.2 Youth Commitment and Forming Social Mentalities:

Drawing in the young inside networks is significant for molding social perspectives towards creature government assistance. Instructive projects, local area effort, and drives that affect youngsters in protection endeavors can add to a change in social qualities over the long haul. This segment examines the job of youth commitment in impacting social advancement.

5.3 Exhibiting Positive Social Practices:

Featuring positive instances of social practices that line up with creature government assistance standards can rouse change. This includes displaying occasions where networks have effectively coordinated social customs with moral treatment of creatures, filling in as models for other people. This part investigates the likely effect of highlighting positive social practices.

9.3 Emerging technologies and their impact on animal welfare

The quick headway of innovation has achieved remarkable open doors and difficulties in different spaces, remembering its effect for creature government assistance. Arising advances can possibly upset how we collaborate with, care for, and grasp creatures. In any case, this progress additionally raises moral contemplations in regards to the utilization of innovation in manners that might affect the prosperity of creatures. This investigation digs into the different scene of arising innovations and their nuanced suggestions for creature government assistance.

Mechanical Advancements in Checking and Grasping Creature Conduct

1.1 GPS Following and Development Nature:

Worldwide Situating Framework (GPS) following has empowered analysts to concentrate on the development examples and conduct of creatures in their normal environments. This innovation is especially valuable for protection endeavors, assisting researchers with understanding relocation courses, natural surroundings inclinations, and the effect of ecological changes on creature conduct. This segment investigates how GPS following adds to natural life examination and preservation.

1.2 Biologging Gadgets and Bioinformatics:

Biologging gadgets, for example, creature borne sensors, gather huge measures of information on a singular creature's physiological and natural boundaries. Combined with progressions in bioinformatics, this innovation offers experiences into the wellbeing, feelings of anxiety, and by and large prosperity of creatures. This segment examines the expected advantages and moral contemplations of involving biologging gadgets for creature government assistance research.

1.3 AI in Conduct Examination:

AI calculations can dissect complex standards of conduct, giving a more profound comprehension of creature conduct. This innovation helps with perceiving indications of pain, sickness, or strange way of behaving, adding to early intercession for hostage and wild creatures the same. This segment investigates how AI adds to conduct examination and its moral ramifications.

Veterinary Medication and Clinical Developments

2.1 Telemedicine for Distant Interviews:

Telemedicine has changed veterinary consideration by empowering distant discussions and diagnostics. This innovation is especially significant in remote or distant regions, giving opportune clinical help to natural life, domesticated animals, and pets. This part looks at the positive effect of telemedicine on creature wellbeing and government assistance.

2.2 Progressions in Veterinary Imaging:

Mechanical developments in imaging, for example, attractive reverberation imaging (X-ray) and processed tomography (CT) filters, offer nitty gritty bits of knowledge into the life structures and wellbeing of creatures. These progressions help in precise diagnostics and treatment arranging, limiting obtrusive techniques. This segment investigates how veterinary imaging advances add to worked on creature government assistance.

2.3 Genomic Medication and Accuracy Reproducing:

Progresses in genomics have prepared for accuracy rearing, considering designated hereditary alterations to improve positive characteristics in creatures. While this innovation holds potential for illness opposition and further developed government assistance, moral worries emerge in regards to unseen side-effects and the potential for double-dealing. This part looks at the moral contemplations encompassing genomic medication and accuracy rearing.

Man-made consciousness in Creature Farming

3.1 Accuracy Domesticated animals Cultivating:

Accuracy Domesticated animals Cultivating (PLF) uses sensors, information examination, and man-made consciousness (computer based intelligence) to screen the wellbeing and prosperity of domesticated animals. This innovation means to improve cultivating rehearses, decrease natural effect, and upgrade animal government assistance on ranches. This segment investigates the expected advantages and moral difficulties of carrying out PLF in creature farming.

3.2 Mechanized Checking in Creature Farming:

Mechanization advances, like automated frameworks and sensors, are progressively utilized in creature cultivation. These developments screen taking care of, draining, and generally wellbeing, limiting human-creature clashes and further developing proficiency. This segment examines the effect of computerized checking on creature government assistance and addresses likely moral worries.

3.3 computer based intelligence in Creature Conduct Forecast:

Man-made consciousness can foresee animal way of behaving in view of broad datasets, permitting ranchers to expect issues connected with wellbeing, generation, and by and large prosperity. This innovation expects to give early mediation and work on creature government assistance in agrarian settings. This segment investigates the capability of artificial intelligence in foreseeing and upgrading creature conduct.

Difficulties and Moral Contemplations

4.1 Protection and Intrusive Observing:

Mechanical developments frequently include intrusive observing techniques, raising worries about the protection and independence of creatures. This segment talks about the moral contemplations encompassing the utilization of observing advancements that might barge in on a creature's regular way of behaving or undermine its protection.

4.2 Potentially negative side-effects of Hereditary Control:

Accuracy rearing and hereditary adjustment might have unseen side-effects, for example, medical problems or the deficiency of hereditary variety. This part investigates the moral difficulties related with hereditary control, stressing the significance of capable and moral utilization of these advances.

4.3 The Advanced Separation in Veterinary Consideration:

While telemedicine has extended admittance to veterinary consideration, a computerized partition exists, restricting access for certain networks or people without sufficient innovative assets. This segment tends to the difficulties of guaranteeing fair admittance to veterinary administrations and the likely moral ramifications of this gap.

Moral Rules and Guideline

5.1 Laying out Moral Systems:

The joining of arising innovations into creature government assistance rehearses requires the foundation of clear moral systems. This includes considering the prosperity, independence, and normal ways of behaving of creatures while carrying out innovative arrangements. This part investigates the significance of moral rules in directing the utilization of innovation in creature government assistance.

5.2 Administrative Oversight and Responsibility:

Legislative and worldwide administrative bodies assume a critical part in supervising the moral utilization of arising advances in creature government assistance. Laying out and upholding guidelines guarantees responsibility and forestalls the abuse of innovation that might hurt creatures. This part talks about the meaning of administrative oversight in keeping up with moral guidelines.

5.3 Cooperation with Partners:

Creating and carrying out moral rules requires coordinated effort among different partners, including researchers, veterinarians, creature government assistance associations, and networks. This part investigates the significance of comprehensive dynamic cycles that consolidate different points of view to address the moral ramifications of arising advancements.

Public Mindfulness and Instruction
6.1 Expanding Public Mindfulness:
Teaching the general population about the positive effect of arising advancements on creature government assistance, as well as the possible moral worries, is fundamental. This segment investigates the job of public mindfulness crusades and instructive drives in encouraging comprehension and capable utilization of innovation in creature care.

6.2 Teaching Experts in Creature Sciences:
Experts in animal sciences, including veterinarians, specialists, and homestead administrators, need far reaching schooling on the moral contemplations of utilizing arising advances. This part examines the significance of incorporating moral preparation into instructive projects to guarantee capable and educated use regarding innovation.

6.3 Empowering Moral Advancement:
Advancing moral advancement includes empowering specialists and innovation engineers to focus on creature government assistance in their plans. This segment investigates the job of motivations, grants, and moral plan rivalries in encouraging a culture of dependable development in arising advancements.